USGBC LEED AP Homes Study Guide

Copyright

Copyright © 2009 by the U.S. Green Building Council. All rights reserved.

The U.S. Green Building Council, Inc. (USGBC) devoted significant time and resources to create this Study Guide. USGBC authorizes individual use of the Study Guide. In exchange for this authorization, the user agrees:

(1) to retain all copyright and other proprietary notices contained in the Study Guide,

(2) not to sell or modify the Study Guide, and

(3) not to reproduce, display, or distribute the Study Guide in any way for any public or commercial purpose, including display on a website or in a networked environment.

Unauthorized reproduction or display of the Study Guide violates copyright, trademark, and other laws and is prohibited. Redistributing the Study Guide on the internet or otherwise reproducing and/or distributing the Study Guide is STRICTLY prohibited even if offered free of charge.

Disclaimer

Using the Study Guide does not guarantee a successful outcome on the examination which is the subject of this Study Guide. The Study Guide is provided as-is with no warranty of any kind, either expressed or implied, including, but not limited to, the implied warranties of merchantability and fitness for a particular purpose. Use of the concepts, examples and information is at the user's own risk. USGBC does not take any responsibility for damages that may arise from the use of the Study Guide. The Study Guide is not associated with nor endorsed by the Green Building Certification Institute. The knowledge needed to pass the exam should come from a variety of sources including hands-on experience, instructor-led courses, the relevant LEED Rating System and the related LEED reference guide. The Study Guide is intended to help users structure their study efforts.

As a condition of use, the user covenants not to sue and agrees to waive and release the U.S. Green Building Council, Inc., its officer, directors and volunteers from any and all claims, demands, and causes of action for any injuries, losses, or damages (including, without limitation, failure to pass any Green Building Certification Institute examination) that the user may now or hereafter have a right to assert against such parties as a result of the use of, or reliance on, the Study Guide.

U.S. Green Building Council

2101 L Street, NW
Suite 500
Washington, DC 20037

Trademark

LEED® is a registered trademark of the U.S. Green Building Council.

ISBN: 978-1-932444-25-4

USGBC LEED AP Homes Study Guide Acknowledgments:

The USGBC LEED AP Homes Study Guide is a valuable tool for exam candidates planning to attain the Homes Specialty. We would like to extend our deepest gratitude to those involved in the production of this resource.

PROJECT TEAM

Green Building Services, Inc. (GBS)

Caitlin Francis, *Project Manager*

Glen Phillips, *Technical Specialist*

Katrina Shum Miller, *Principal in Charge*

Earth Advantage

Katie Schnepp, *Homes Educational Coordinator*

Randy Hansell, *Homes Specialist and Developer*

NonObvious Solutions

Elizabeth Gast, *Technical Illustrator and Graphic Designer*

Eric von Schrader, *Instructional Designer*

Prometric

Examination Question Writing Training

LEED Curriculum Committee Members

Draft reviews

USGBC Staff

Karol Kaiser, *Director of Education Development*

Jacob Robinson, *Project Manager*

HOMES OVERVIEW

The Leed AP Homes Credential Overview	1
Getting Started on Your LEED for Homes Credential	2
About the Exam	4
Exam Content Areas	4
Exam Questions	5
Practice Questions	6
Study Tips	6
Exam Day Tips	7

GREEN BUILDING WITHIN LEED FOR HOMES

The Rundown	9
The Process	11
The Players	12
Universal Requirements for Participation	14
Eligible Project Types	15
The Other Particulars	17
Home Size Adjustment	17
Accountability Forms	17
Certification Process	17
LEED for Homes Sampling Protocol	18
Credit Interpretation Requests and Innovation & Design Requests	18
LEED for Homes General Key Terms	21

INNOVATION & DESIGN

What About Innovation & Design?	23
ID Overview	24
ID Synergies	24
ID Credits	25
ID Key Terms	25
ID Credit Summaries	26
ID Category Review	44
ID Learning Activities	45
ID Practice Questions	46

LOCATION & LINKAGES

What About Location & Linkages?	47
LL Overview	48
LL Synergies	48
LL Credits	49
LL Key Terms	50
LL Credit Summaries	52
LL Category Review	68
LL Learning Activities	69
LL Practice Questions	70

SUSTAINABLE SITES

What About Sustainable Sites? 71
SS Overview 72
SS Synergies 73
SS Credits 73
SS Key Terms 74
SS Credit Summaries 76
SS Category Review 102
SS Learning Activities 103
SS Practice Questions 104

WATER EFFICIENCY

What About Water Efficiency? 105
WE Overview 106
WE Synergies 107
WE Credits 107
WE Key Terms 108
WE Credit Summaries 110
WE Category Review 124
WE Learning Activities 125
WE Practice Questions 126

ENERGY & ATMOSPHERE

What About Energy & Atmosphere? 127
EA Overview 128
EA Synergies 129
EA Credits 130
EA Key Terms 131
EA Credit Summaries 134
EA Category Review 170
EA Learning Activities 171
EA Practice Questions 172

MATERIALS & RESOURCES

What About Materials & Resources? 173
MR Overview 174
MR Synergies 175
MR Credits 175
MR Key Terms 176
MR Credit Summaries 178
MR Category Review 196
MR Learning Activities 197
MR Practice Questions 198

INDOOR ENVIRONMENTAL QUALITY

What About Indoor Environmental Quality?	199
EQ Overview	200
EQ Synergies	201
EQ Credits	202
EQ Key Terms	203
EQ Credit Summaries	204
EQ Category Review	250
EQ Learning Activities	251
EQ Practice Questions	252

AWARENESS & EDUCATION

What About Awareness & Education?	253
AE Overview	254
AE Synergies	255
AE Credits	255
AE Key Terms	255
AE Credit Summaries	256
AE Category Review	264
AE Learning Activities	265
AE Practice Questions	266

APPENDIX

Practice Question Answer Key	267
Credit Review Sheet	271
Acronyms and Organizations	271
Exemplary Performance Matrix	274
Reference Standard Table	276
LEED for Homes Simplified Checklist	279
LEED for Homes Accountability Form	280
LEED for Homes Durability Risk Evaluation Form	281
LEED for Homes Durability Inspection Checklist	282

CREDENTIAL OVERVIEW

This study guide is a resource that can help you prepare for the LEED AP Homes Examination. It summarizes the critical points of the LEED for Homes Rating System in an easy-to-review format. So you can master the content, it also includes a variety of study tools, including review questions, learning activities, and practice questions that use the same format as the actual exam.

Congratulations on your decision to pursue the LEED AP Homes credential. You are positioning yourself within the marketplace as a professional who is committed to keeping up with current trends and best practices.

As you prepare for the exam, you will be taking what you already know about LEED and green building, and developing greater proficiency in an area that is specific and relevant to your line of work.

Accreditation will certify you have the knowledge and skills necessary to participate in the LEED application and certification process, hold a firm understanding of green building practices and principles, and are familiar with LEED requirements, resources, and processes.

Best of luck on the exam!

GETTING STARTED ON YOUR LEED AP HOMES CREDENTIAL

Earning the LEED AP Homes credential requires passing a two-part exam:

PART 1: (Also the Green Associate Credential) A two-hour exam. Passing Part 1 attests to the candidate's knowledge of good environmental practice and skill, and reflects understanding and support of green design, construction and operations. If you have already earned the Green Associate credential, you only need to take Part 2 of the LEED AP for Homes exam. (Go to the GBCI website, www.gbci.org for details).[1]

PART 2: A two-hour exam. Passing Part 2 attests that the candidate possesses the knowledge and skills necessary to participate in the design process, to support and encourage integrated design, and to streamline the application and certification process.[2]

You must pass Part 1 before you can take Part 2. You may take both parts of the exam on either the same day or on separate days.

STEP 1: **Read** the *LEED® AP LEED for Homes Candidate Handbook* at www.gbci.org to determine if you meet the eligibility requirements.

STEP 2: **Register** for and schedule your exam.

Tips: Register in the EXACT name that appears on your I.D. card, and keep your confirmation number.

STEP 3: **Access** the reference documents.

The Candidate Handbook lists the primary and ancillary references that are the sources for exam questions. Some references are available for free download, and others can be purchased at www.usgbc.org.

Note that exam reference documents are subject to change as the GBCI exams evolve. Always check the candidate handbooks for the most up-to-date list of reference documents.

Exam Part 1 (Green Associate):

Review the references listed in the Candidate Handbook and consider purchasing the *Green Building and LEED Core Concepts Guide, 2008 Edition* from USGBC. This core resource is now packaged to include the Study Guide for LEED Green Associate!

Exam Part 2 (Homes):
References:

- *LEED for Homes Reference Guide, 2008*, U.S. Green Building Council (available for purchase at www.usgbc.org/store).

---

1   *LEED AP Homes Candidate Handbook* (GBCI, 2009)
2   *LEED AP Homes Candidate Handbook* (GBCI, 2009)

- *LEED for Homes Rating System* (USGBC, 2008).

- *Summary of Changes to LEED for Homes for Mid-Rise Buildings*, (USGBC, 2008).

- *LEED for Neighborhood Development Pilot Rating System: Neighborhood Pattern and Design* (USGBC, 2008).

- *Energy Star Qualified Homes Thermal Bypass Inspection Checklist* (US Environmental Protection Agency; www.epa.gov).

- *Introduction to Indoor Air Quality: About Carbon Monoxide Detectors* (US Environmental Protection Agency; www.epa.gov/iaq/co.html).

- "*Making Your House Quieter*," by Spike Carlson (The Family Handyman, April 2000).

You should also be familiar with the content of the U.S. Green Building Council's Website, www.usgbc.org, including but not limited to LEED Project Registration, LEED Certification content, and the purpose of LEED Online. The U.S. Green Building Council's LEED Website, www.usgbc.org/leed, also has free access to LEED Rating Systems, LEED Reference guide Introductions, and Checklists beyond those listed above.

STEP 4: Start studying!

Have all of the reference documents available as you work through this study guide, most importantly the LEED for Homes Reference Guide, 2008.

The LEED AP Homes Examination is rigorous and challenging, so you need more than this guide to prepare yourself fully. Be sure to also study the essential resources listed above.

Important Note: A 2009 Edition of LEED for Homes Reference Guide is now available, however, exam items are written from the LEED for Homes Reference Guide, 2008 Edition. GBCI will give a three-months notice before incorporating exam items using the 2009 Edition reference guide. You should refer to the appropriate edition listed in the Candidate Handbook to prepare for the exam.

LEED AP HOMES CREDENTIAL

The Exam has eight major areas of focus that are called out in the Candidate Handbook. Here is how they align with the Rating System credit categories:

GBCI EXAM AREAS OF FOCUS	LEED RATING SYSTEM CREDIT CATEGORIES
I. Project Site Factors =	Sustainable Sites (SS) Location & Linkages (LL)
II. Water Management =	Water Efficiency (WE) Sustainable Sites (SS)
III. Project Systems and Energy Impacts =	Energy & Atmosphere (EA)
IV. Acquisition, Installation, and Management of Project Materials =	Materials & Resources (MR)
V. Improvements to the Indoor Environment =	Indoor Environmental Quality (EQ) Materials & Resources (MR)
VI. Stakeholder Involvement in Innovation =	Innovation & Design (ID) Awareness & Education (AE)
VII. Project Surroundings and Public Outreach =	Location & Linkages (LL) Sustainable Sites (SS)

II. Exam Questions

GBCI exam questions are:

- Developed and validated by global work groups of subject matter experts;

- Referenced to current standards and resources;

- Developed and monitored through psychometric analysis; and

- Designed to satisfy the test development specifications of a job analysis.

The questions assess your knowledge at three levels:

- **Recall questions** test the candidate's direct knowledge of concepts. This section may require the test taker to define terms or concepts, recall facts, recognize or identify components or steps in a process, and group items into categories.

- **Application questions** evaluate the test taker's knowledge of procedures and performance and may require the candidate to demonstrate how things work, perform calculations following a formula, place components or steps into proper sequence, describe how a process works, and apply a known process or sequence of actions to accomplish a task (such as troubleshooting a problem using a detailed checklist).

- **Analysis questions** test the candidate's reasoning and problem-solving abilities. Such questions may require the candidate to demonstrate an understanding of how things work, cause and effect, and underlying rationale; analyze problems and devise appropriate solutions; build a conceptual model of a process; troubleshoot a problem without a checklist; and analyze and solve a problem.

Questions follow consistent formats:

- You will likely never see an "all of the above," "none of the above," "true/false" or "what is the best?" type of question on this test, because:
    - These questions can cause confusion and have overlapping answers.
    - The test is intended to be clear and straightforward.
    - The question language is never intended to be tricky.

- You will likely never see a credit number listed by itself; any direct reference to a LEED credit will include the full credit name.

- Most acronyms are spelled out so that you do not need to memorize all acronyms you learn.
    - Commonly referenced acronyms may be used (i.e. LEED, ASHRAE, and VOC), so it is still a good idea to know what these acronyms stand for!

- You will see some questions with multiple correct answers (for example, a question prompting the reader to "select two" responses).

- While this is not a math test, you will need to have a good understanding of the required calculations and equations associated with compliance to LEED prerequisites and credits. The Prometric center will have a built-in calculator on the computer screen for you to use during the exam. No outside calculators will be permitted.

PRACTICE QUESTIONS IN THIS STUDY GUIDE

Practice questions in this guide were written by subject matter experts trained by Prometric using the same guidelines as the actual item writers for the examinations. These sample questions will allow you to become familiar with exam expectations, format and question type. This should improve your testing skills and alleviate stress on test day, allowing you to focus on core information.

STUDY TIPS

You will learn best if you establish a regular study schedule over a period of time. Daily studying in shorter sessions is more effective for most people than "cramming" in long sessions at the last minute.

Studying with a partner or a group can help you stay on schedule and give you opportunities to quiz and drill with each other.

Here's a step-by-step approach for using your study resources:

- Read the LEED for Homes Reference Guide, 2008, one category at a time. Don't try to learn everything on your first pass.

- Read the corresponding section in this study guide.

- Take notes and highlight key points.

- Review the other reference materials that apply to this category.

- Reread the reference guide category.

- Utilize the review questions, learning activities, and practice questions in this guide.

- Keep reviewing and rereading until you are confident you know the material.

EXAM DAY TIPS

General Strategies

- Always arrive early and take a moment to relax and reduce your anxiety.
  - This brief time period will boost your confidence.
  - Use this time to focus your mind and think positive thoughts.

- Plan how you will use the allotted time.
  - Estimate how many minutes you will need to finish each test section.
  - Determine a pace that will ensure that you complete the whole test on time.
  - Don't spend too much time on each question.

- Maintain a positive attitude.
  - Don't let more difficult questions raise your anxiety and steal your valuable time. Move on and find success with other questions.
  - Avoid watching for patterns. Noticing that the last four answers are "c" is not a good reason to stop, go back, and break concentration.

- Rely on your first impressions.
  - The answer that comes to mind first is often correct.
  - Nervously reviewing questions and changing answers can do more harm than good.

- Plan to finish early and have time for review.
  - Return to difficult questions you marked for review.
  - Make sure you answered all questions.

Multiple Choice Strategies

- Formulate your own answer before reading the options.
  - Look down from the question and see if you can answer it without looking at the options. Focus on finding an answer without the help of the alternative options.
    - This process will increase your concentration.
    - Doing this will help you exercise your memory.

- Read all the choices before choosing your answer.

- Eliminate unlikely answers first.

- Eliminating two alternatives quickly may increase your probability to 50-50 or better.

- Look for any factor that will make a statement false.
  - It is easy for the examiner to add a false part to an otherwise true statement.
  - Test takers often read the question and see some truth and quickly assume that the entire statement is true. For example, "Water boils at 212 degrees in Denver." Water does boil at 212 degrees, but not at Denver's altitude.

- Beware that similar answers provide a clue. One of them is correct; the other is disguised.
  - This is likely not a trick, but make sure you know the exact content being asked.
- Consider the answers carefully. If more than one answer seems correct for a single-answer question:
  - Ask yourself whether the answer you're considering completely addresses the question.
  - If the answer is only partly true or is true only under certain narrow conditions, it's probably not the right answer.
  - If you have to make a significant assumption in order for the answer to be true, ask yourself whether this assumption is obvious enough that everyone would make it. If not, ignore that answer.
- If you suspect that a question is a trick item, make sure you're not reading too much into the question, and try to avoid imagining detailed scenarios in which the answer could be true. In most cases, "trick questions" are only tricky because they're not taken at face value.
  - The test questions will only include relevant content and are not intended to trick you or test your reading ability.

GREEN BUILDING WITHIN

LEED FOR HOMES

THE RUNDOWN

- LEED for Homes differs from other commercial LEED Rating Systems in ways it is rated, administered, and structured.

- All prerequisites must be met—they are mandatory!

- The devil is in the details—candidates should know the Rating System thoroughly!

- Not all credits can be earned on every project.

- Most credits are prescriptive—detailed calculations are the exception, not the rule.

- LEED for Homes is not part of the LEED 2009 Rating Systems.

- LEED for Homes does not use LEED Online.

Prerequisites	18
Credits	67
Possible Points	136

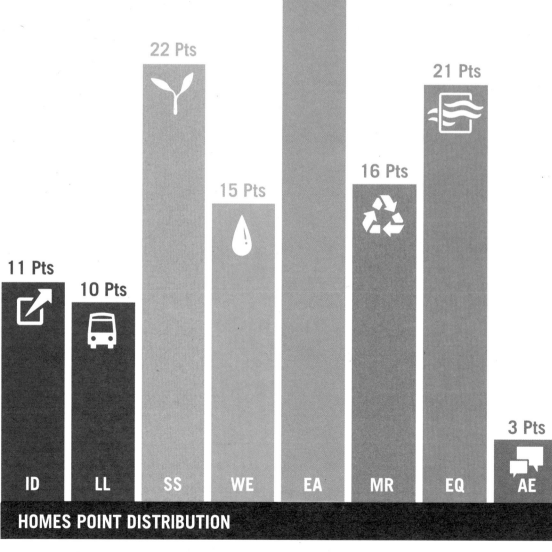

11 Pts
10 Pts
22 Pts
15 Pts
38 Pts
16 Pts
21 Pts
3 Pts

ID | LL | SS | WE | EA | MR | EQ | AE

HOMES POINT DISTRIBUTION

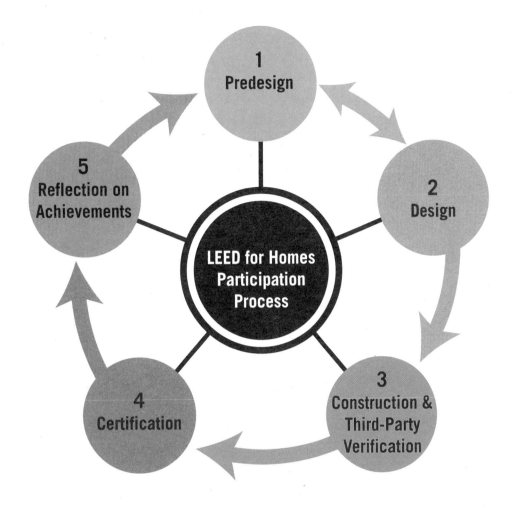

THE PROCESS: Five Steps to Participate

STEP 1.   Predesign: Contact a LEED for Homes Provider and join the program

- The project team selects and engages a LEED for Homes Provider.
- Register the project with USGBC.

STEP 2.   Design: Identify a project team

- Identify the project team that will plan, design and build the home.
- The project team will determine the specific goals, strategies, and systems required to meet those goals.
- The Provider or Green Rater will assist the project team.

STEP 3.   Construction and third-party verification: Build the home

- The project team builds the home to achieve the desired level of performance.
- The Green Rater conducts visual inspections of various measures in the home and either performs or arranges for the required and optional performance tests to be conducted.

STEP 4. Certification: Certify the home

The certification process involves two components:

- First, is the field inspection and performance testing. The Green Rater conducts a final inspection and conducts the required performance tests. The Green Rater then completes the project documentation package and submits it to the LEED for Homes Provider for review and approval. The package includes:
  - A completed and signed LEED for Homes Checklist;
  - Completed and signed Accountability Forms; and
  - A completed and signed Durability Risk Evaluation Form and durability inspection checklist.
- Second, the Provider reviews the project documentation package submitted by the Green Rater. If it is satisfactory, the Provider forwards the project documentation package to USGBC for final review and certification.

STEP 5. Reflection on Achievements

- Builders and project teams that are registered with LEED for Homes may market their LEED-certified homes with USGBC-approved press releases, signage and collateral pieces that highlight the LEED brand. Some projects may be driven by the home buyer, in which case this step is irrelevant.

THE PLAYERS

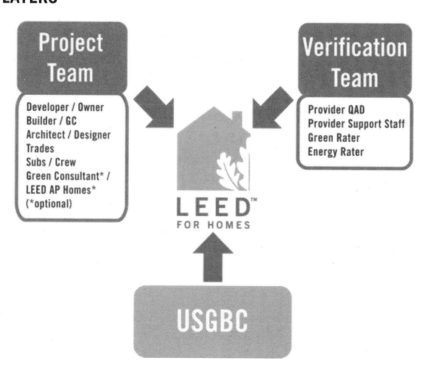

Project Team

- Contact a LEED for Homes Provider and register the project.
- Identify the project team and select green features for the home.
- Build a quality home!
- Address concerns and questions.
- Reflect on the team's achievements, and market the home.

Verification Team

- Promote the LEED for Homes initiative.
- Conduct a preliminary review of the home's current design.
- Provide quality assurance oversight of Green Raters.
- Conduct verification and performance testing.
- Complete appropriate documentation.
- Conduct a certification review with USGBC.

LEED for Homes Provider

The USGBC has created a network of LEED for Homes Providers to deliver the program in local markets across the country. Providers are local organizations with documented experience and expertise in their region's market. They help builders register projects, perform the preliminary review of a project's LEED documentation, conduct the quality assurance review of project documents, submit documents necessary for certification to USGBC, provide green home rating support services to building teams, and, train, coordinate, and oversee a network of green raters.

LEED for Homes Green Rater

The LEED for Homes program uses a verification expert called a LEED for Homes Green Rater. This individual has experience and expertise in conducting field verification and performance testing of LEED for Homes measures. The Green Rater is responsible for working with project teams to verify project measures and completing the project documentation package that is then submitted to the Provider's Quality Assurance Designee for review prior to final submittal to USGBC for the certification review.

USGBC

- Educate LEED for Homes Providers and Green Raters.
- Maintain the Rating System standards.
- Maintain a database of registered projects.
- Provide quality assurance oversight of Providers.
- Certify projects.
- Maintain a database of certified projects.
- Provide marketing tool kits.

UNIVERSAL REQUIREMENTS FOR PARTICIPATION

To participate in LEED for Homes, a project:

- **Must be defined as a "dwelling unit," per LEED for Homes.** This means that every participating home must have a cooking area and a bathroom.

- **Must have Provider involvement.** Projects that have begun construction prior to contacting a Provider may participate in LEED for Homes subject to the judgment of a Provider, as long as all mandatory measures (prerequisites) in LEED for Homes can be met.

- **Must have one LEED for Homes Certification per individual building.** This requirement has the following implications:
  - A building cannot be partially certified. Single units in multifamily buildings cannot participate in LEED for Homes unless the entire building is registered to participate. All stacked living units are considered multifamily buildings.
  - Every unit within a multifamily building must earn the same certification level (for example, Silver, Gold, and so on).
  - Separate buildings must be certified separately. Multiple buildings in a complex, or single-family homes in a subdivision, may be certified separately, but it is not required that all the buildings or homes be certified or that they meet the same certification level. Single-family side-by-side attached homes, such as row houses, are considered separate buildings.

Single-Family Homes

Low-Rise Multifamily

Mid-Rise Pilot Homes

Production Homes

Gut Rehab

ELIGIBLE PROJECT TYPES

The following project types are eligible to participate, subject to the conditions described below:

Detached Single-Family Homes	Conventional single-family homes, whether custom, production or affordable, are eligible to participate.
Attached Single-Family Homes	Homes that serve one family but share one or more vertical party walls with other homes are eligible to participate. This category includes townhomes but does not include stacked duplexes or triplexes, which are considered multifamily buildings.
Low-Rise Multifamily Buildings	Low-rise multifamily buildings are one to three stories high and include two or more dwelling units.
Mid-Rise Multifamily Buildings	Mid-rise multifamily buildings are defined as buildings with four to six stories and at least two dwelling units. These projects are allowed to participate in the LEED for Homes Mid-rise Pilot, which will run through 2010. Mid-rise projects must follow the guidance laid out in the Mid-rise Addendum to LEED for Homes, which includes special energy modeling and ventilation requirements. In order to participate in the Mid-rise Pilot, each project must have (a) adequate expertise to conduct modeling per ASHRAE Standard 90.1; and (b) adequate expertise on mid-rise components and systems so as to provide useful advice on energy-reduction strategies.
Gut/ Rehabilitation Projects	Projects that are characterized as "substantial gut/rehab" can participate in LEED for Homes, as long as all of the prerequisites can be met. In order to qualify as a substantial gut/rehab, a project must replace most of its systems and components (for example, HVAC or windows) and must open up the exterior walls to enable the thermal bypass inspection to be completed.
Manufactured and Modular Housing	Manufactured or modular homes can participate in LEED for Homes, but manufacturing plants cannot be LEED certified; only individual homes can earn certification, and only after the home is constructed on-site. Providers and Green Raters are encouraged to ensure that all of the energy requirements are met, particularly the thermal bypass inspection (see EA Prerequisite 1.1, Performance of ENERGY STAR for Homes). These projects will generally require the involvement of the plant manager or owner, and Providers may need to arrange on-site plant inspections.
Mixed-Use Buildings	Mixed-use projects may participate if at least 50% of the building's total floor area is residential. In these cases, the project team is expected to prepare "green" tenant fit-out guidelines that address the energy, water, air quality and materials performance of the nonresidential portion of the building. These guidelines can be based on the commercial LEED Rating Systems.

Dormitories and Assisted Living Facilities	These buildings are typically identified by the presence of a central kitchen facility and the fact that they fall outside the scope of ASHRAE Standard 62.2. Any building of this type that does not have cooking and bathroom facilities cannot participate in LEED for Homes. If each unit has its own cooking area and bathroom, the building should be treated as a multifamily building. Buildings with central kitchen facilities must fall into one of the following categories: • Small buildings, with two to nine units: These buildings should be treated as single-family homes, and each unit should be treated as a separate bedroom. • Larger buildings, with 10+ units: These buildings should be treated as multifamily buildings, in which each unit is a separate living unit and each unit is compartmentalized (that is, isolated from common spaces and each other). In this case, central kitchens and common bathrooms are required to meet the local exhaust requirements in ASHRAE Standard 62.1. Common living spaces are required to meet the ventilation requirements in ASHRAE Standard 62.1. In-unit spaces are still required to meet the ventilation requirements in ASHRAE Standard 62.2.
International Projects	At this time, projects outside the United States, U.S. territories, or military bases are not allowed to participate in LEED for Homes, with the exception of projects in Canada. Canadian projects are allowed to participate because USGBC is working with the Canadian Green Building Council to develop a program in Canada.
"In-Law" Flats	In-law units are typically small, separate units that are attached to or co-located with single-family homes. There are a few different designs for in-law flats: • Attached, with a shared entrance or interior connections (such as doors): The in-law flat should be treated as part of the main home. The flat may be considered a separate bedroom, but not a separate unit. • Attached, with a separate entrance: The in-law flat must earn the same certification as the main home, but it can be treated as either a separate unit or an additional bedroom to the main home. • Detached: The in-law flat is a separate building from the main home, and the project team can choose whether to pursue LEED certification.

THE OTHER PARTICULARS

There are other basic elements involved in LEED for Homes certification that are good to know and aren't addressed in any one specific credit but are integral to the entire rating system.

Home Size Adjustment:

It's pretty straightforward - larger homes typically consume more materials during construction and typically use more energy to provide comfort over the home's life cycle than will a smaller home.

The Home Size Adjustment compensates for these effects by making it easier or harder to reach each LEED for Homes award level. There is no impact on the award threshold for an average sized home, whereas thresholds for smaller-than-average homes are lower and those for larger-than-average homes are raised.

Table 4 Homes Reference Guide, First Edition 2008. Introduction, page 10. Threshold Adjustment (point range: −10 to +10)

Maximum home size (ft²) by number of bedrooms					Adjustment to award thresholds*
≤ 1 bedroom	2 bedrooms	3 bedrooms	4 bedrooms	5 bedrooms	
610	950	1290	1770	1940	−10
640	990	1340	1840	2010	−9
660	1030	1400	1910	2090	−8
680	1070	1450	1990	2180	−7
710	1110	1500	2060	2260	−6
740	1160	1570	2140	2350	−5
770	1200	1630	2230	2440	−4
800	1250	1690	2320	2540	−3
830	1300	1760	2400	2640	−2
860	1350	1830	2500	2740	−1
900	**1400**	**1900**	**2600**	**2850**	**0 ("neutral")**
940	1450	1970	2700	2960	+1
970	1510	2050	2810	3080	+2
1010	1570	2130	2920	3200	+3
1050	1630	2220	3030	3320	+4
1090	1700	2300	3150	3460	+5
1130	1760	2390	3280	3590	+6
1180	1830	2490	3400	3730	+7
1220	1910	2590	3540	3880	+8
1270	1980	2690	3680	4030	+9
1320	2060	2790	3820	4190	+10
For larger homes or homes with more bedrooms, see below.					

Example: An adjustment of −5 means that the threshold for a Certified LEED Home is 40 points (rather than 45 points for an average-sized home). Silver certification would require a minimum of 55 points rather than 60 points, Gold would require a minimum of 70, and Platinum, 85.

Many measures in the LEED for Homes Rating System have a substantial design component or may be difficult for the Green Rater to visually verify. The LEED for Homes Accountability Form is used for such measures. The professional who designed and installed such measures assumes responsibility for compliance with the requirements by signing an Accountability Form. The form shifts the responsibility for verification from the Green Rater to the professional responsible for that specific measure. See the Appendix section for a sample Accountability Form.

The certification process includes two components.

I. Field inspection performed by the Green Rater and a performance testing that can be performed by the Green Rater or a qualified Home Energy Rating System (HERS) Rater. The result of this field verification and performance testing is the completion of the project documentation package, which is then sent to the LEED for Homes Provider.

II. LEED for Homes Provider confirms that the project documentation package is complete and submits it to USGBC for certification.

LEED FOR HOMES SAMPLING PROTOCOL

For projects that have a high volume of homes being built, a LEED for Homes Sampling Protocol can be used. This applies to large-volume single-family and low-rise multifamily projects and enables production and low-rise multifamily builders to reduce certification costs if they are able to demonstrate consistency in their construction practices.

CREDIT INTERPRETATION REQUESTS AND INNOVATION & DESIGN REQUESTS

Credit Interpretation Requests (CIRs) are questions about whether designs, technologies or practices will meet the "intent" of a given LEED for Homes credit (and thereby be awarded LEED points). USGBC-approved CIRs provide an alternate compliance pathway for a given credit, when the builder cannot meet the requirements stated in the rating system for that credit.

Innovation & Design (ID) Process Requests are questions about whether designs, technologies or practices that are not currently included in the LEED for Homes Rating System can be awarded LEED points and/or whether exceptional performance above the requirements set by the LEED for Homes Rating System can be awarded LEED points. USGBC-approved ID Requests provide a method for a builder to receive credit for including an innovative new measure or exceptional performance that is beyond the scope of the existing rating system.

When Should CIRs and ID Requests Be Submitted?

Builders are encouraged to submit project-related CIRs and IDs to their Provider as early as possible (at the time of the preliminary rating).

STEP 1: Informal evaluation of the CIR or ID Request

When a builder submits a question or ID Request to the Provider, the Provider should:

- Conduct a quick assessment of whether the CIR or proposed ID Request has previously been resolved by searching the LEED for Homes CIR/ID Database.

- If the CIR or ID Request has not previously been resolved, contact the LEED for Homes technical consultant to inquire about the proposed CIR or ID Request.

If the CIR or ID Request has previously been resolved, the technical consultant will respond accordingly. Otherwise, the consultant may ask for a formal CIR or ID Request, with more supporting information and/or data.

STEP 2: Formal CIR or ID Request submittals

- Formal CIRs or ID Requests should be submitted to USGBC. USGBC will acknowledge receipt of the request within one to two days and forward the request to the relevant Technical Advisory Sub-Committee (TASC). Each CIR and ID Request will also be given a database identification number (for example, EA 03-12).

Credit Interpretation Requests

All CIRs should clearly explain the following:

- Primary points of concern or confusion;
- Any proposed alternative approach or interpretation; and
- Type of information or clarification needed to resolve the question.

ID Requests

All ID Requests should include information similar to the structure of all LEED for Homes credits:

- Proposed intent;
- Proposed measures; and
- Proposed metric.

- Verification/submittals.
- Proposed benefits: This should include an explanation of how the proposed measures will yield environmental, human health or other benefits, and an estimate of the net benefits compared with:
  - Standard building practices; and
  - Other LEED for Homes credits.

An explanation of how the estimate was calculated must also be included. Wherever possible, the team should provide references to published material, including third-party research (preferred) and/or manufacturers' estimates.

Most ID Requests will be judged using metrics similar to those used to justify existing LEED for Homes credits. Table 1 provides a list of sample metrics, as well as a rough evaluation of how performance within each metric is rewarded by LEED for Homes.

Table 1: Sample Metrics and Benchmarks for Environmental Performance

Sample Intent	Sample Metric for Performance	Typical LEED for Homes Benchmarks for Performance
Reduced energy use	Percentage of total annual energy use	3% reduction in total annual energy use*
Reduced water use	Percentage of total annual water use	5% reduction in total water use*
Reduced waste	Percentage of total waste diverted	25% reduction in material waste to landfill*
Reduced material	Square footage of wood	1,000–1,500 square feet of wood
Improved air quality	Health risk	Substantially reduced human health risks
* All percentages refer to the savings achieved compared with performance in a conventional home, not a green home.		

STEP 3: Evaluation of the CIR or ID Request

- All formal CIRs and ID Requests will be reviewed and resolved by either a TASC or USGBC staff member.

STEP 4: Formal response

Once a final resolution has been made, the technical consultant does the following:

- Records the resolution in the database;
- Relays the resolution to the questioning Provider; and
- Incorporates any changes into future versions of the Rating System.

LEED FOR HOMES GENERAL KEY TERMS

bedroom	In LEED for Homes, any room or space that could be used or is intended to be used for sleeping purposes and meets local fire and building code requirements.
Credit Interpretation Request (CIR)	CIRs are questions about whether designs, technologies or practices will meet the "intent" of a given LEED for Homes credit (and thereby be awarded LEED points). USGBC-approved CIRs provide an alternate compliance pathway for a given credit when the builder cannot meet the "requirements" stated in the rating system for that credit.
exemplary performance	The exceeding of the requirements for a credit already awarded in the LEED for Homes Rating System. The requirements for earning exemplary performance credit are listed for each credit in the LEED for Homes Reference Guide, 2008. Exemplary performance credit is not available on each credit but is typically reserved for credits where exceeding the current requirements will yield a substantial environmental or human health benefit.
Green Rater	An individual who performs field inspections and performance testing of LEED for Homes measures for the LEED for Homes Provider. A HERS rater with additional training can become a LEED for Homes Green Rater.
project	The design and construction of a LEED-certified home. A project may include multiple homes in a development.
Provider	An organization that recruits, trains and coordinates LEED for Homes Green Raters to serve as third-party verifiers of LEED-certified homes. Providers are the official certifiers of LEED for Homes on behalf of the U.S. Green Building Council.
Quality Assurance Designee (QAD)	An individual who works for a LEED for Homes Provider who has the responsibility for ensuring that the LEED for Homes quality assurance program is implemented at the Provider level.
Innovation & Design (ID) Requests	Questions about whether designs, technologies or practices that are not currently included in the LEED for Homes Rating System can be awarded LEED points and/or whether exceptional performance above the requirements set by the LEED for Homes Rating System can be awarded LEED points. USGBC-approved ID Requests provide a method for a builder to receive credit for including an innovative new measure or exceptional performance that is beyond the scope of the existing rating system. USGBC-approved IDs most likely will become LEED for Homes credits in the next version of the rating system.
Technical Advisory Sub-Committee	In LEED for Homes, a group of specialists who rule on Credit Interpretation Requests and Innovation and Design Process Requests.

NOTES...

INNOVATION & DESIGN

The Innovation & Design (ID) category, known as "Innovation in Design" in the updated 2009 Edition rating system, provides an opportunity to project teams to pursue new technologies and methods that greatly exceed the existing requirements of the LEED Rating Systems or that are not addressed by any prerequisite or credits. Innovation credits must demonstrate quantifiable energy, environmental or human health benefits.

WHAT ABOUT INNOVATION & DESIGN?

What potential benefits do you see in a brainstorming session with experts in all of the following fields?

Residential building design, mechanical engineering, energy engineering, performance testing, sustainable design, civil engineering, landscape architecture, habitat restoration and land use planning.

What low-cost strategies could be considered during design to improve the durability of the home?

INNOVATION & DESIGN

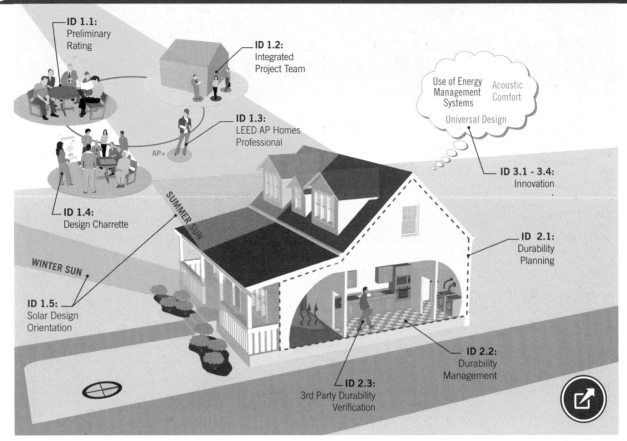

ID 1.1: Preliminary Rating

ID 1.2: Integrated Project Team

ID 1.3: LEED AP Homes Professional

AP+

ID 1.4: Design Charrette

SUMMER SUN

WINTER SUN

ID 1.5: Solar Design Orientation

Use of Energy Management Systems — Acoustic Comfort — Universal Design

ID 3.1 - 3.4: Innovation

ID 2.1: Durability Planning

ID 2.2: Durability Management

ID 2.3: 3rd Party Durability Verification

THE OVERVIEW

Sustainable design strategies and measures are constantly evolving and improving. New technologies are continually introduced to the marketplace, and up-to-date scientific research influences building design strategies. Occasionally, a strategy results in building performance that greatly exceeds that required in an existing LEED credit. Other strategies may not be addressed by any LEED prerequisite or credit but warrant consideration for their sustainability benefits.

SYNERGIES

The prerequisites and credits of this section are intended to promote an integrated, system-oriented approach to project design and development. The selected home-building strategies and technologies in the Rating System should each be fully integrated into a home's design.

Many of the credits in the Rating System can serve as durability strategies and may be used in the creation of a durability inspection checklist. If this is done, the home can still receive LEED points for those credits. Also, think about how Integrated Project Planning can impact all of the processes, techniques, materials, and equipment during the design, construction, and operation of the home.

Throughout the Rating System you should pay attention to the credits that are eligible for exemplary performance. A project can receive points for exceeding the performance requirements of existing credits. Last, this section also rewards innovative or regional measures that are not addressed elsewhere in the Rating System.

ID

THE CREDITS

ID 1: Integrated Project Planning	These credits are intended to promote an integrated, systems-oriented approach to green project design and development.
ID 2: Durability Management Process	These credits are designed to inspire builders to examine project-specific durability concerns and seek site-appropriate solutions to mitigate the highest durability risks.
ID 3: Innovative or Regional Design	These credits encourage project teams to investigate and possibly earn points for implementing strategies or measures that are not addressed in the current LEED for Homes Rating System.

KEY TERMS

charrette	An intensive, collaborative session in which a project team discusses design and construction options related to all aspects of the home.
durability	The ability of a building or any of its components to perform their required function in their service environment over a period of time without unforeseen cost for maintenance or repair.
Green Rater	An individual who performs field inspections and performance testing of LEED for Homes measures for the LEED for Homes Provider. A HERS rater with additional training can become a LEED for Homes Green Rater.
Provider	An organization that recruits, trains and coordinates LEED for Homes Green Raters to serve as third-party verifiers of LEED-certified homes. Providers are the official certifiers of LEED for Homes on behalf of the U.S. Green Building Council.
Technical Advisory Sub-Committee	In LEED for Homes, a group of specialists who rule on Credit Interpretation Requests and Innovation and Design Process Requests.

PRIMARY BENEFITS

- Early coordination of the project for all building trades will lead to a greater understanding of the project goals and the requirements needed to be met by project staff and will help the team better achieve the project owner's goals.

STANDARDS

None

INTENT

Maximize opportunities for integrated, cost-effective adoption of green design and construction strategies.

REQUIREMENTS

- Conduct a preliminary rating meeting with the LEED for Homes Provider and key members of the project team to determine the targeted LEED award level, the measures being pursued and who is responsible for each credit.

IMPLEMENTATION

- Key members of the project team need to meet with the LEED for Homes Provider or their designee to determine the level of performance and credits that are to be pursued.

- Better safe than sorry! Once a certification goal has been established, plan to earn approximately five or more points more than necessary so the goal can still be met if several measures are not attained during construction.

VERIFICATION & SUBMITTALS

PROJECT TEAM

- Participate in the preliminary rating meeting.

GREEN RATER

- Participate in the preliminary rating meeting or verify Provider participation in the meeting.

DOCUMENTATION & CALCULATIONS

None

TIMELINE/TEAM

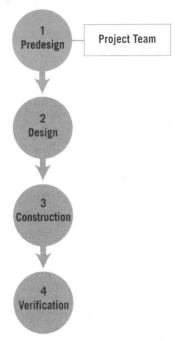

1 Predesign — Project Team

2 Design

3 Construction

4 Verification

NOTES

- The project team should strive to have a good understanding of the LEED for Homes Rating System and how to achieve the measures.

1 Point

ID 1: Integrated Project Planning
ID Credit 1.2: Integrated Project Team

PRIMARY BENEFITS

- Helps to promote the "Home as a system" approach.
- Helps keep the project on track.
- Identifies problems early so they can be addressed as soon as possible.

STANDARDS

None

INTENT

Maximize opportunities for integrated, cost-effective adoption of green design and construction strategies.

REQUIREMENTS

- The integrated project team must include, at a minimum, three skill sets.
- The team is to be involved in a minimum of three phases of the home design and construction process.
- The team must meet at least monthly to review project progress.

IMPLEMENTATION

- Assemble a qualified project team that will be involved in an iterative design process. This team can consist of skilled individuals who have a wide range of experience and are able to help develop an integrated, systems approach to the design and construction of the project.
- The Green Rater is not to be counted as one of the integrated project team members.
- The three skill sets can reside in two individuals if they are qualified with each skill.

VERIFICATION & SUBMITTALS

PROJECT TEAM

● Present a list of project team members to the Green Rater.

● Present a list of meeting dates or plans for regularly scheduled meetings to the Green Rater.

GREEN RATER

● Visually verify the list of project team members.

DOCUMENTATION & CALCULATIONS

None

TIMELINE/TEAM

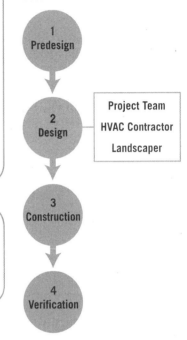

NOTES

● An individual who works for the Provider can be counted as a member of the integrated project team if he or she has been hired separately to provide consulting services and does not provide any verification services on the project.

1 Point | **ID 1: Integrated Project Planning, ID Credit 1.3: Professional with the LEED AP for Homes Credential**

PRIMARY BENEFITS

- Involving a LEED AP Homes in the project can help the team integrate measures into the project.

STANDARDS

LEED AP Homes designation

INTENT

Maximize opportunities for integrated, cost-effective adoption of green design and construction strategies.

REQUIREMENTS

- One principal member of the project team must hold the LEED AP Homes designation.

- The preceding individual must not be a member of the verification team.

- The LEED AP Homes credential must have been earned and verified by the Green Rater prior to the project's preliminary meeting.

IMPLEMENTATION

- The individual who serves as the LEED AP Homes for the project cannot be on the verification team. This includes any individual in the Provider organization who is involved with the verification services and the Green Rater.

- Projects must have the LEED AP Homes involved from the preliminary rating through the design and construction of the project to claim this point.

VERIFICATION & SUBMITTALS

PROJECT TEAM

- Identify the LEED AP Homes to the Green Rater.

GREEN RATER

- Verify the participation of the LEED AP Homes on the project team.

DOCUMENTATION & CALCULATIONS

None

TIMELINE/TEAM

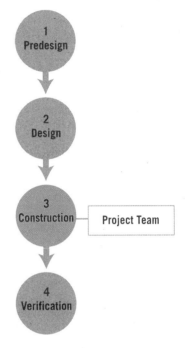

NOTES

- At least one principal member of the project team shall be a professional who holds the LEED AP Homes designation.

1 Point

ID 1: Integrated Project Planning
ID Credit 1.4: Design Charrette

PRIMARY BENEFITS

- Assists the project team in exploring and addressing a number of strategies regarding creating coordinated design and construction of the project.

- Promotes an integrated, systems approach to the project. The outcome is a home that has integrated a holistic strategy into its design and construction.

STANDARDS

None

INTENT

Maximize opportunities for integrated, cost-effective adoption of green design and construction strategies. The charrette is intended to integrate the green strategies across all aspects of building design.

REQUIREMENTS

- Conduct at least a full-day integrated design charrette workshop no later than the design development phase with the project team.

- Team members must include, at a minimum, three skill sets.

IMPLEMENTATION

- The design charrette cannot take place later than the design development phase.

- The charrette may be conducted as multiple half-day charrettes if the entire project team is involved and receives the approval of the Provider and Green Rater.

VERIFICATION & SUBMITTALS

PROJECT TEAM

- Present information about the charrette (dates, participants and so on) to the Green Rater.

GREEN RATER

- Participate in the charrette, or verify project team members' participation in the charrette.

DOCUMENTATION & CALCULATIONS

None

TIMELINE/TEAM

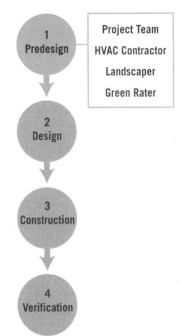

1 Predesign	Project Team
	HVAC Contractor
2 Design	Landscaper
	Green Rater
3 Construction	
4 Verification	

NOTES

- Although not required, it is suggested that the Green Rater or the Provider participate in the design charrette.

PRIMARY BENEFITS

- The home is designed to take advantage of solar opportunities in the future.

STANDARDS

None

INTENT

Maximize opportunities for integrated, cost-effective adoption of green design and construction strategies.

REQUIREMENTS

- Design the home to incorporate a number of solar design strategies:

  ○ Glazing on the north- and south-facing walls is at least 50% greater than the sum of glazing of the east- and west-facing walls.

  ○ The east–west axis of the building is within 15 degrees of due east–west.

  ○ The roof has a minimum of 450 square feet of south-facing area that is oriented appropriately for solar application.

  ○ At least 90% of the glazing on the south-facing wall is completely shaded at noon on June 21 and unshaded on December 21.

IMPLEMENTATION

- Solar design needs to take place as early as possible, because changing the design may become costly later.

VERIFICATION & SUBMITTALS

PROJECT TEAM

- Present any calculations or simulation results to the Green Rater.

GREEN RATER

- Visually verify that calculations or simulations were performed to meet the credit requirements.

- Visually verify any relevant design elements (for example, trees, overhangs, awnings).

DOCUMENTATION & CALCULATIONS

Four calculations are required for this measure:

- Determine the ratio of the glazing area on the north and south-facing walls.

- Calculate the precise location of the home.

- Calculate the area of the roof that is south-facing.

- Calculate the glazing shading in summer and the lack of shading in winter.

TIMELINE/TEAM

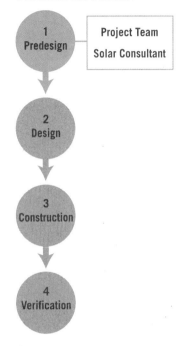

1 Predesign — Project Team, Solar Consultant

2 Design

3 Construction

4 Verification

NOTES

- Project teams that plan on using additional solar strategies beyond this measure should use the Performance Pathway of the Energy & Atmosphere category.

PRIMARY BENEFITS

• All homes face risks where they are built. Addressing these risks will improve both the life of the measures and the home.

STANDARDS

None

INTENT

Promote durability and high performance of the building enclosure and its components and systems through appropriate design, materials selection and construction practices.

REQUIREMENTS

Conduct a durability evaluation of the site where the home will be built to assess the risks. Develop strategies to address any risks found. Do the following:

1. Complete the Durability Risk Evaluation Form to identify all moderate- and high-risk durability issues for the building enclosure.

2. Develop specific measures to respond to those issues. For issues that have received a moderate- or high-risk rating, a minimum of three durability strategies need to be developed.

3. Identify and incorporate all the applicable indoor moisture-control measures listed in Table 1 on page 37 of the LEED for Homes Reference Guide, 2008.

4. Incorporate the measures in steps 2 and 3 above into the project documents.

5. List all the durability measures and indicate their locations in the project documents in a durability inspection checklist. Include the checklist in project documents for use in verification.

IMPLEMENTATION

● Bring key members of the project team together and meet and evaluate the durability risk factors that a home faces at a specific site.

● Incorporate strategies into the home design to address the risks.

● Consider using credits in the rating system in other ways; many of the credits can serve as durability strategies and may be used in the creation of the durability inspection checklist.

IMPLEMENTATION, CONTINUED

- Consider using the durability templates developed by USGBC (recommended).

- Remember, the principal durability risks are:

  - Exterior water;
  - Interior moisture loads;
  - Air infiltration;
  - Interstitial condensation;
  - Heat loss;
  - Ultraviolet radiation;
  - Pests; and
  - Natural disasters.

VERIFICATION & SUBMITTALS

PROJECT TEAM

- Complete and submit the Durability Risk Evaluation Form to the Green Rater.

- Include durability measures in project documents.

- Develop and submit a completed durability inspection checklist.

GREEN RATER

- Verify completion of the Durability Risk Evaluation Form and the durability inspection checklist.

DOCUMENTATION & CALCULATIONS

None

TIMELINE/TEAM

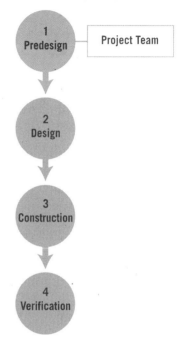

1 Predesign — Project Team

2 Design

3 Construction

4 Verification

NOTES

- USGBC and its representatives are responsible only for verifying the completion of LEED for Homes requirements; such verification in no way constitutes a warranty as to the appropriateness of the selected durability measures or the quality of implementation.

PRIMARY BENEFITS

- All homes face risks where they are built. Addressing those risks will improve the life of the home and the measures incorporated in the home.

STANDARDS

None

INTENT

Promote durability and high performance of the building enclosure and its components and systems through appropriate design, materials selection and construction practices.

REQUIREMENTS

- The builder must develop a quality assurance process to ensure that the selected durability measures are installed in the home.

IMPLEMENTATION

- By working with the necessary trades, incorporate into the construction of the home the durability strategies developed during the durability risk evaluation phase in ID 2.1.

- Develop and use a durability inspection checklist.

- Consider using the durability templates provided by USGBC (recommended).

VERIFICATION & SUBMITTALS

PROJECT TEAM

● Present the Green Rater with documentation of the quality management processes. Conduct an inspection of the durability measures in the home, indicating the completion of the inspection on the durability inspection checklist.

GREEN RATER

● Visually verify documentation of the quality management processes, or verify that the project team conducted an on-site inspection of the durability measures and indicated its completion on the durability inspection checklist.

DOCUMENTATION & CALCULATIONS

A completed durability inspection checklist.

TIMELINE/TEAM

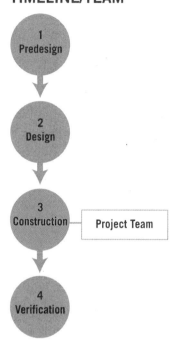

NOTES

● USGBC and its representatives are responsible only for verifying the completion of LEED for Homes requirements; such verification in no way constitutes a warranty as to the appropriateness of the selected durability measures or the quality of implementation.

PRIMARY BENEFITS

- The Green Rater offers another set of eyes to verify that the selected measures have been incorporated into the home.

STANDARDS

None

INTENT

Promote durability and high performance of the building enclosure and its components and systems through appropriate design, materials selection and construction practices.

REQUIREMENTS

- The Green Rater or qualified third-party takes the durability plan developed in ID 2.1 and verifies that each measure has been incorporated into the home during construction.

- The Green Rater or qualified third-party must verify that each measure on the durability inspection checklist has been implemented.

IMPLEMENTATION

- Have a third party verify the durability measures.

VERIFICATION & SUBMITTALS

PROJECT TEAM

- Present the durability inspection to the Green Rater to conduct the verification inspection.

GREEN RATER

- Visually verify that strategies listed on the durability inspection checklist were incorporated into the home.

- Upon verification, check off and sign the durability inspection checklist.

DOCUMENTATION & CALCULATIONS

None

TIMELINE/TEAM

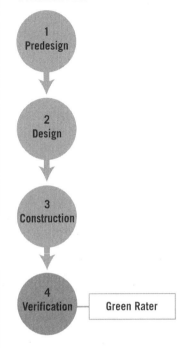

NOTES

None

PRIMARY BENEFITS

- New strategies, technologies and measures are always being developed in the housing industry. The Innovative or Regional Design credits encourage the adoption of new measures that will improve the energy and environmental performance of the home.

STANDARDS

None

INTENT

Minimize the environmental impact of the home by incorporating additional green design and construction measures that have tangible and demonstrable benefits beyond those in the LEED for Homes Rating System.

REQUIREMENTS

- Determine whether a strategy, measure or product has an energy-related or environmental impact on the home or the home lot for which the LEED for Homes Rating System awards no points.

- Develop an ID Request under the guidance of the LEED for Homes Provider.

- This section recognizes exemplary performance measures used throughout the rating system.

IMPLEMENTATION

- Determine at the start of the project whether any innovative or exemplary performance measures will be attempted.

- Submit any ID Requests at the earliest opportunity, to allow the project team to find out whether the proposed measure(s) will be allowed to earn points.

VERIFICATION & SUBMITTALS

PROJECT TEAM

- Notify the LEED for Homes Provider as early as possible about any intent to submit an ID Request.

- Complete a formal Innovative Design or Regional Design Request and submit to the Provider.

GREEN RATER

- Review the Innovative Design or Regional Design Request.

- Submit the request to USGBC for review.

- Provide feedback to the project team about the ruling.

DOCUMENTATION & CALCULATIONS

- Calculations may be required for this measure if the project team is pursing an ID Request that has energy or water savings.

TIMELINE/TEAM

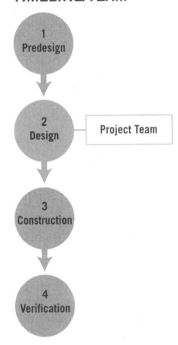

1 Predesign

2 Design — Project Team

3 Construction

4 Verification

NOTES

- The project team meets with the LEED for Homes Provider or the Provider's representative to determine whether any applicable innovative strategies are being incorporated into the home that are not recognized in the LEED for Homes Rating System.

- Only LEED for Homes Providers may submit an ID Request to USGBC.

- ID points cannot be counted until LEED for Homes has ruled on the request.

- Exemplary performance measures are recognized in this section.

- Only four points are available in this section. They can be earned through a combination of Innovative Design or Regional and exemplary performance measures.

1 List some of the skill sets that could be included in an integrated project team for a LEED for Homes project.

_____

_____

2 What are the principal durability risk factors that should be considered when developing a durability management plan?

_____

_____

3 How would a design charrette have benefited your last project?

_____

_____

4 Make a list of some regional environmental or human health concerns in your area.

_____

_____

Conduct an informational interview with a project manager or consultant in the green building field or audit a design charrette to learn more about the integrated project team approach.

ASK AROUND

Visit the Building America website, www.eere.energy.gov/buildings/building_america.

Download a free, climate-specific Best Practices Guide that includes detailed information about design and construction practices that follow building science principles.

FIND OUT MORE

Conduct an informational interview with a green architect or green builder to learn about the significant durability risks that must be considered when building homes in your area.

ASK AROUND

1 A home's location on the site and its orientation should be determined in the earliest phases of the project for which of the following reasons?

    A) Decisions regarding location and orientation can be very time consuming.

    B) Site location and orientation affect all other aspects of design and construction.

    C) Early determination of site and orientation are required by financial institutions.

    D) Orientation of the site can affect wildlife and natural areas.

2 What do you need to include in an innovative design request?

    A) Project schedule and owner name

    B) Estimated project cost and completion date

    C) Photographs and narrative

    D) The intent and proposed benefits

3 Exemplary performance credit is different than innovative design credit in that exemplary performance credit is ___?

    A) earned by implementing a technology that is not currently in the LEED for Homes Rating System.

    B) available for every credit.

    C) earned by exceeding the requirements of specific existing credits.

    D) automatically awarded for similar strategies in future projects at the time it is awarded for one project.

4 Which of the following is considered a principal durability risk?

    A) An underground pool

    B) Faulty plumbing

    C) Proximity of site to a wetland

    D) Interior moisture loads

See Answer Key on page 267.

LOCATION & LINKAGES

The Location & Linkages (LL) category addresses where we build our homes. The locations and sites that are selected for homes are critical decisions that affect wildlife habitats and agricultural and natural resource lands. This category rewards builders for choosing building sites that avoid environmentally sensitive sites or contain precious resources.

WHAT ABOUT LOCATION & LINKAGES?

How can the location of a home reduce dependence on personal automobiles?

What strategies can limit the amount of new infrastructure required for a project site?

How can prime farmland be protected from development?

LOCATION & LINKAGES

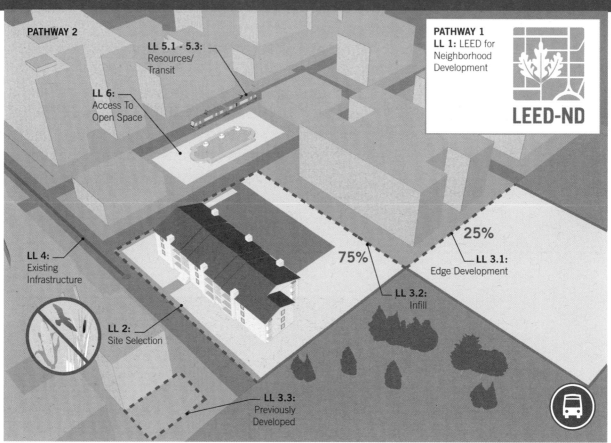

THE OVERVIEW

Location & Linkages addresses site-related environmental effects, in terms of both the impact to the site itself and the impact that stems from the location of the site. This section describes how best to choose site locations that promote environmentally responsible land-use patterns and neighborhoods.

SYNERGIES

The credits in this section are closely related to each other to help home builders create an integrated approach to selecting appropriate sites for homes. Think about how to integrate the principles of smart growth and pedestrian-oriented design in housing developments. Develop a process to evaluate potential housing sites that incorporates among other strategies, more efficient use of land, reduced fragmentation of farmland and wilderness, reduced needs for infrastructure development and provide an opportunity for a wide selection of transit and pedestrian-friendly options.

LOCATION & LINKAGES

This category has been developed in conjunction with the LEED for Neighborhood Development program. Many of the strategies and measures in both efforts will overlap. Project teams may want to review the LEED for Neighborhood Development program for additional opportunities to integrate measures into their housing development, and you may want to review the LEED for Neighborhood Development Rating System to identify the commonalities.

THE CREDITS

LL

The LEED credits in this section reward builders for selecting homesites that have more sustainable land-use patterns than, and offer environmental advantages over, conventional developments.

There are two pathways to achieve these credits:

Pathway 1	
LL 1: LEED for Neighborhood Development	This credit recognizes project teams that choose to build their homes in neighborhoods certified under LEED for Neighborhood Development.
	LEED for Neighborhood Development is designed to certify communities that emphasize environmentally responsible planning and layout of the infrastructure and buildings that together constitute a neighborhood. The Location & Linkages section recognizes that there are synergies between the LEED for Neighborhood Development program and the LEED for Homes program.

OR

Pathway 2—LL 2–6:	
LL 2: Site Selection	This credit rewards project teams for choosing building sites that avoid environmentally sensitive areas or contain precious resources.
LL 3: Preferred Locations	This credit promotes the efficient use and reuse of land and minimized alteration of previously undeveloped land by encouraging project teams to locate projects in environmentally preferable locations.
LL 4: Infrastructure	This credit rewards the selection of a homesite within a community that has existing municipal water and sewer lines.
LL 5: Community Resources/Transit	This credit rewards projects located near abundant local community resources or mass transit options.
LL 6: Access to Open Space	This credit rewards project teams that select a homesite that is located near publicly accessible open space or that include open space in a multi-home development.

KEY TERMS

development	The homes and building lots that surround the LEED for Homes project that is to be built.
disturbed lot area	The part of a site that is directly affected by construction activity, including any activity that would compact the soil or damage vegetation.
edge development	Generally, a group of homes that extend an existing community beyond its borders but remain connected to it. In LEED for Homes, at least 25% of an edge development's perimeter must border land that has been previously developed.
infill site	A lot in an existing community. In LEED for Homes, an infill site is defined as having at least 75% of its perimeter bordering land that has been previously developed.
lot	The individual parcel of land on which a home is to be built.
previously developed land	Having pre-existing paving, construction or significantly altered landscapes. This does not apply to altered landscapes resulting from current agricultural use, forestry use or use as preserved natural area.
previously developed site	In LEED for Homes, a lot consisting of at least 75% previously developed land.
prime farmland	Land that has the best combination of physical and chemical characteristics for producing food, feed, forage, fiber, and oilseed crops, and is also available for these uses. (U.S. CFR, Title 7, Part 657.5).
site	The individual building lot where a home is to be built. A site may include all of the lots that a builder is responsible for.
subdivision	The homes and building lots that immediately surround the new LEED for Homes project that is to be built. A subdivision may be new or pre-existing, and belongs to a larger development.

wetland	An area inundated or saturated by surface or ground water at a frequency and duration sufficient to support, and that under normal circumstances does support, a prevalence of vegetation typically adapted for life in saturated soil conditions (U.S. Code of Federal Regulations, Title 40, Part 232). Wetlands generally include swamps, marshes, bogs and similar areas.

10 Points | **LL 1: LEED for Neighborhood Development**
LL Credit 1: LEED for Neighborhood Development

PRIMARY BENEFITS

- Uses land efficiently.

- Reduces spread of development.

- Reduces need for infrastructure.

- Increases opportunity for community resources to be developed and utilized.

STANDARDS

LEED for Neighborhood Development Rating System.

INTENT

Minimize the environmental impact of land development practices by building homes in LEED for Neighborhood Development–certified developments.

REQUIREMENTS

- Complete the requirements of the LEED for Neighborhood Development certification program.

IMPLEMENTATION

- Examine the LEED for Neighborhood Development Rating System for opportunities to integrate this system with the LEED for Homes Rating System.

VERIFICATION & SUBMITTALS

PROJECT TEAM

- Demonstrate LEED for Neighborhood Development certification.

GREEN RATER

- Verify LEED for Neighborhood Development certification.

DOCUMENTATION & CALCULATIONS

None

TIMELINE/TEAM

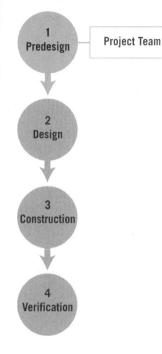

NOTES

- A project earning points for LL 1 is not eligible for points under LL 2–6, and vice versa.

- Projects do not need to complete LEED for Neighborhood Development certification before earning these points, but the requirements of LEED for Neighborhood Development Stage 2 must be met.

PRIMARY BENEFITS

- Preserves sensitive habitat.

- Potentially preserves wetlands.

STANDARDS

U.S. Code of Federal Regulations 40 CFR, Parts 230–233 and Part 22.

State Natural Resources Conservation Service soil surveys, www.nrcs.usda.gov/about/organization/regions.html.

Visit http://websoilsurvey.nrcs.usda.gov/app/ for soil survey area information by state and county.

INTENT

Avoid development on environmentally sensitive sites.

REQUIREMENTS

Meet all of the following:

- Do not build on land below the 100-year floodplain.

- Do not build on land identified as habitat for any species on federal or state threatened or endangered lists.

- Do not build on land within 100 feet of any water.

- Do not build on land that prior to acquisition was public farmland, unless land of equal value or greater value as parkland is accepted in trade.

- Do not build on land that contains prime soils, unique soils or soils of state significance.

IMPLEMENTATION

- Conduct research to ensure that all the requirements are being met.

- Involve professionals in land development or a similar field in the development of this measure.

VERIFICATION & SUBMITTALS

PROJECT TEAM

- Review soil and site data.

- Sign an Accountability Form confirming that the site meets all the stipulations of the credit.

GREEN RATER

- Verify that the Accountability Form has been signed by the responsible party.

DOCUMENTATION & CALCULATIONS

- At least 95% of the site must meet the requirements for each listed requirement above.

- This measure earns no points or 2 points.

TIMELINE/TEAM

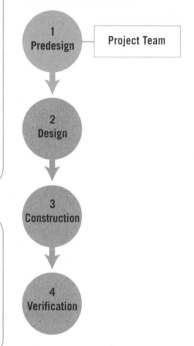

1 Predesign — Project Team

2 Design

3 Construction

4 Verification

NOTES

- A project earning points for LL 1 is not eligible for points under LL 2–6, and vice versa.

1 Point | **LL 3: Preferred Locations**
LL Credit 3.1: Edge Development Site

PRIMARY BENEFITS

- Reduces the impact on the environment.

- Encourages the development and use of community resources.

- Allows for efficient use of existing infrastructure such as water, sewer and roads.

STANDARDS

None

INTENT

Encourage the building of LEED-certified homes near or within existing communities.

REQUIREMENTS

- Select a lot such that at least 25% of the perimeter of the project site immediately borders previously developed land.

IMPLEMENTATION

- Select land that borders existing development.

VERIFICATION & SUBMITTALS

PROJECT TEAM

- Present any relevant calculations to the Green Rater.

GREEN RATER

- Visually verify that calculations are complete and satisfy the credit requirements;

  and/or

- Visually verify that the site meets the credit requirement.

DOCUMENTATION & CALCULATIONS

- Calculate the percentage of the perimeter that borders previously developed land.

TIMELINE/TEAM

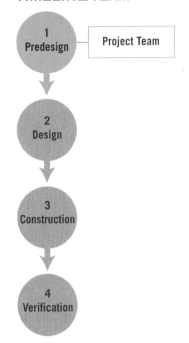

1 Predesign — Project Team

2 Design

3 Construction

4 Verification

NOTES

- Any fraction of the perimeter that borders waterfront is excluded from the total perimeter.

- Previously developed land must have development on it that is at least 5 years old.

- Previously developed land must have development on it that is immediately adjacent to the LEED project.

- A project can claim the points only for LL 3.1 or LL 3.2.

- A project earning points for LL 1 is not eligible for points under LL 2–6, and vice versa.

2 Points | **LL 3: Preferred Locations**
LL Credit 3.2: Infill Site

PRIMARY BENEFITS

- Reduces the impact on the environment.

- Encourages the development and use of community resources.

- Allows for efficient use of existing infrastructure such as water, sewer and roads.

STANDARDS

None

INTENT

Encourage the building of LEED-certified homes near or within existing communities.

REQUIREMENTS

- Select a lot such that at least 75% or more of the perimeter immediately borders previously developed land.

IMPLEMENTATION

- Select land that borders existing development.

VERIFICATION & SUBMITTALS

PROJECT TEAM

● Present any relevant calculations to the Green Rater.

GREEN RATER

● Visually verify that calculations are complete and satisfy the credit requirements;

and/or

● Visually verify that the site meets the credit requirement.

DOCUMENTATION & CALCULATIONS

● Calculate the percentage of the perimeter that borders previously developed land.

TIMELINE/TEAM

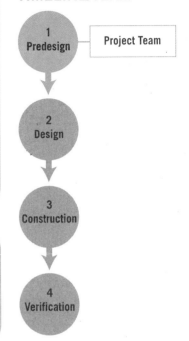

1 Predesign — Project Team

2 Design

3 Construction

4 Verification

NOTES

● Any fraction of the perimeter that borders waterfront is excluded from the total perimeter.

● Previously developed land must have development on it that is at least 5 years old.

● Previously developed land must have development on it that is immediately adjacent to the LEED project.

● A project can claim the points only for LL 3.1 or LL 3.2.

● A project earning points for LL 1 is not eligible for points under LL 2–6, and vice versa.

1 Point | **LL 3: Preferred Locations**
LL Credit 3.3: Previously Developed Site

PRIMARY BENEFITS

- Reduces the impact on the environment by using previously developed land.

- Encourages the development and use of existing community resources.

- Allows for efficient use of existing infrastructure such as water, sewers and roads.

STANDARDS

None

INTENT

Encourage the building of LEED-certified homes near or within existing communities.

REQUIREMENTS

- At least 75% of the site was previously developed by having preexisting paving, construction or altered landscapes.

- Landscapes altered by current agricultural use, forestry use, or use as a preserved natural area do not count as previously developed areas.

IMPLEMENTATION

- Select land that was previously developed.

VERIFICATION & SUBMITTALS

PROJECT TEAM

- Present any relevant calculations to the Green Rater.

GREEN RATER

- Visually verify that calculations are complete and satisfy the credit requirements;

  and/or

- Visually verify that the site meets the credit requirement.

DOCUMENTATION & CALCULATIONS

- Calculate the percentage of the land that has been previously developed.

TIMELINE/TEAM

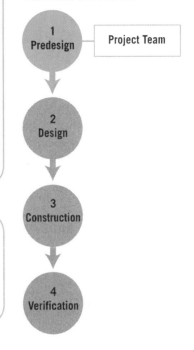

NOTES

- Previously developed land must have development that is at least 5 years old.

- A project earning points for LL 1 is not eligible for points under LL 2–6, and vice versa.

PRIMARY BENEFITS

- Reduced need for infrastructure development.

- Building a home on a lot that can be connected to existing infrastructure reduces the resources needed to provide basic services to the home.

STANDARDS

None

INTENT

Encourage the building of LEED-certified homes in developments that are served by or are near existing infrastructure (sewers and water supply).

REQUIREMENTS

- Build on a lot that is within one-half mile of existing water service lines and sewer service lines.

IMPLEMENTATION

- Determine which communities have existing infrastructure and develop projects in those areas.

VERIFICATION & SUBMITTALS

PROJECT TEAM

- If necessary, present local maps and documents to the Green Rater demonstrating the proximity of the home to existing water and sewer infrastructure.

GREEN RATER

- Visually verify (using maps, documents or on-site observation) that the home is within one-half mile of existing water and sewer infrastructure.

DOCUMENTATION & CALCULATIONS

- Calculate the distance from the home to the nearest existing water and sewer hookup.

TIMELINE/TEAM

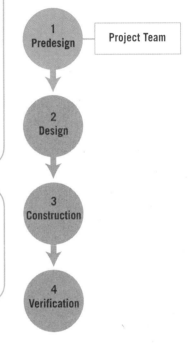

NOTES

- A project earning points for LL 1 is not eligible for points under LL 2–6, and vice versa.

- Even though the infrastructure needs to be within the designated distance, the project is not required to connect to the systems to earn the point.

1 - 3 Points | LL 5: Community Resources/Transit

PRIMARY BENEFITS

- Building homes near community resources or transit provides the opportunity to walk or ride public transit, reducing the need for automobiles.

- Homes that are built near community resources such as restaurants, stores and parks encourage walking or riding of bikes. Likewise, homes that are built near public transit encourage the use of such transportation to travel.

STANDARDS

None

GOOD, BETTER, BEST

LL Credit 5.1: Basic Community Resources/Transit OR
LL Credit 5.2: Extensive Community Resources/Transit OR
LL Credit 5.3: Outstanding Community Resources/Transit

INTENT

Encourage the building of LEED-certified homes in development patterns that allow for walking, biking or public transit use (thereby minimizing dependency on personal automobiles and their associated environmental effects).

REQUIREMENTS

Measure	Project Located Within	
5.1: Basic **(1 point)**	¼ mile of 4 basic community resources	½ mile of transit service that offers 30 or more transit rides per weekday
	½ mile of 7 basic community resources	
5.2: Extensive **(2 points)**	¼ mile of 7 basic community resources	½ mile of transit service that offers 60 or more transit rides per weekday
	½ mile of 11 basic community resources	
5.3: **Outstanding** **(3 points)**	¼ mile of 11 basic community resources	½ mile of transit service that offers 125 or more transit rides per weekday
	½ mile of 14 basic community resources	
List of eligible basic community resources can be found on Table 1 on page 70 of the LEED for Homes Reference Guide.		

IMPLEMENTATION

- Select lots for building that are within the prescribed distances, to take advantage of community resources and transit.

- The distance requirements must be calculated based upon possible walking distances, not as the crow flies.

VERIFICATION & SUBMITTALS

PROJECT TEAM

- Present maps and/or a list of community resources or transit modes to the Green Rater.
- If applicable, present calculations for transit rides to the Green Rater.

GREEN RATER

- Visually verify (using maps, lists provided by the project team, and/or on-site observation) the presence of community resources or transit rides as per the credit requirements.
- If applicable, visually verify calculations for transit rides.

DOCUMENTATION & CALCULATIONS

- Distance to community resources is determined by possible walking distances, not as the crow flies. All obstructions must be taken into consideration.
- Transit rides are calculated as follows:
  - Within a one-half–mile radius, count all the different transit lines that have a stop. Multiple stops on the same transit line count only as one within the half-mile radius. Multiply that number by the number of times the bus passes during a weekday for the number of transit rides. A transit line that travels in different directions counts as separate transit lines for the calculation (for example, a bus traveling north past the home and then the same line traveling south past the home counts as two transit lines).

TIMELINE/TEAM

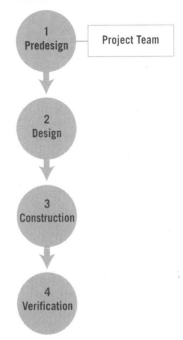

1 Predesign — Project Team

2 Design

3 Construction

4 Verification

NOTES

- A project that has 250 or more transit rides per weekday can earn one ID point under exemplary performance.

- A whole community can qualify for this credit when the distance is measured from the center of the development and the farthest home from that center point does not exceed one-quarter mile.

- A project earning points for LL 1 is not eligible for points under LL 2–6, and vice versa.

1 Point | **LL 6: Access to Open Space**
LL Credit 6: Access to Open Space

PRIMARY BENEFITS

- Homes that have access to open spaces can have smaller yards because the homeowner has access to recreational spaces close to the home.

STANDARDS

None

INTENT

Provide open spaces to encourage walking, physical activity and time spent outdoors.

REQUIREMENTS

- Select a location within one-half mile of a publicly accessible or community-based open space that is at least three-quarters of an acre in size.

- The open-space requirement can be met by either one large open space or two smaller spaces totaling three-quarters of an acre.

IMPLEMENTATION

- Select a site to build that is within the prescribed distance of a qualified open space.

VERIFICATION & SUBMITTALS

PROJECT TEAM

● Present maps and/or directions to the Green Rater.

GREEN RATER

● Visually verify (using maps and/or on-site observation) the presence of open spaces that meet the requirements of the credit.

DOCUMENTATION & CALCULATIONS

● Provide a map or description outlining compliance with the measure.

● Calculate the distance to open space.

● Calculate the size of the accessible open space.

TIMELINE/TEAM

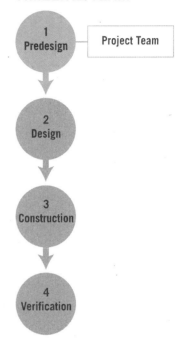

NOTES

● A project earning points for LL 1 is not eligible for points under LL 2–6, and vice versa.

LL CATEGORY REVIEW

1 What are some environmental benefits of building homes on previously developed sites?

_____

_____

2 What are the LEED for Homes definitions of a) infill and b) previously developed land?

_____

_____

3 What are some of the factors that make a site an environmentally sensitive site where development should be avoided?

_____

_____

4 List some of the community resources that can qualify a project for Basic, Extensive or Outstanding Community Resources/Transit.

_____

_____

Development on wetlands or floodplains presents particularly serious environmental challenges because it not only alters wildlife habitats, it can also reduce water quality and increase the likelihood of erosion and flooding. Visit http://msc.fema.gov/webapp/wcs/ > "What are you looking for?" > Flood Maps, to access FEMA issued flood maps for your community. How far are you from a floodplain?

THINK ABOUT IT

To learn more about reduced site disturbance, review the book *Biophilia in Practice: Building that Connect People with Nature.*

Access it from your local library, purchase it through your study group or look up an article that references this book's content from www.BuildingGreen.com.

INVESTIGATE

Evaluate your home (or choose another home in your community) for its proximity to community resources and transit. Would it qualify for any points under Basic Community Resources/Transit, Extensive Community Resources/ Transit, or Outstanding Community Resources/Transit?

WALK AROUND

LL PRACTICE QUESTIONS

1 A detached, single family home is planned for a lot with a water service line that is 1/4 mi (402m) away and a sewer service line that is 3/4 mi (1207 m) away. How many points can be earned for the Existing Infrastructure credit?

A) 0 points

B) ½ points

C) 1 point

D) 2 points

2 The requirement to earn credit LL 3.1, Edge Development is ___?

A) at least 25% of the perimeter immediately borders previously developed land

B) 75% or more of the perimeter borders previously developed land

C) at least 75% of the site was previously developed

D) 100% of the perimeter borders undeveloped, forested land

3 What is the best strategy for meeting the Location & Linkages, Site Selection credit?

A) Develop as far away from a wetland as possible.

B) Closely analyze your budget for cost savings.

C) Build new homes on previously developed infill lots.

D) Construct the home within ½ mile (805 m) of a wetland.

4 Your project site is located within ¼ mile of seven basic community resources. These criteria will earn you 2 points under which of the following credits?

A) Basic Community Resources / Transit

B) Intermediate Community Resources / Transit

C) Extensive Community Resources / Transit

D) Outstanding Community Resources / Transit

5 According to the Access to Open Space credit, open spaces must consist predominantly of softscapes such as ___?

A) private golf courses without deeded public access

B) ponds located within ¾ mile of a walking or bicycle path

C) city or county reservoirs

D) city, county, and state parks

See Answer Key on page 267.

SUSTAINABLE SITES

The design of a site and its natural elements can have a significant environmental impact. The Sustainable Sites (SS) category rewards projects for designing the site to minimize adverse effects on the environment.

WHAT ABOUT SUSTAINABLE SITES?

What are the long- and short-term ecological impacts from residential development? What is the demand for:

Water?

Chemicals?

Pesticides?

What are the ongoing maintenance needs of that site?

What is the urban heat island effect? Why is it significant?

Photo by Hillary Platt

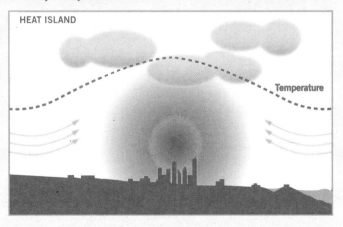

HEAT ISLAND

Temperature

SUSTAINABLE SITES

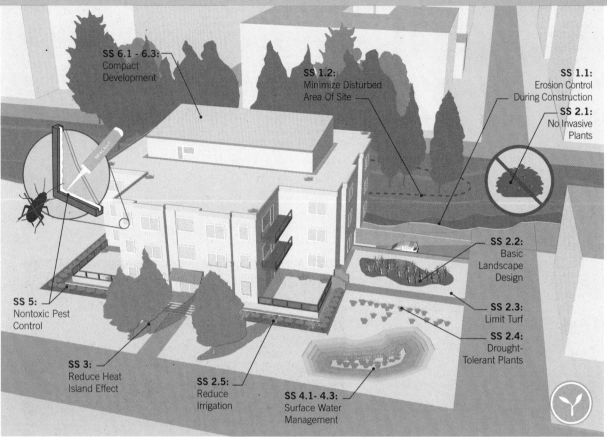

SS 6.1 - 6.3:
Compact Development

SS 1.2:
Minimize Disturbed Area Of Site

SS 1.1:
Erosion Control During Construction

SS 2.1:
No Invasive Plants

SS 2.2:
Basic Landscape Design

SS 5:
Nontoxic Pest Control

SS 2.3:
Limit Turf

SS 2.4:
Drought-Tolerant Plants

SS 3:
Reduce Heat Island Effect

SS 2.5:
Reduce Irrigation

SS 4.1- 4.3:
Surface Water Management

OVERVIEW

Well thought out site design and landscaping decisions can lead to easy to maintain landscaping that protects native plant and animal species and contributes to the health of local and regional habitats.

The way in which a home is, or is not, integrated into the site can have various effects:

- Rain that falls on a site can be either a detriment, by causing soil erosion and runoff of chemicals and pesticides, or a benefit, by offering an opportunity to offset potable water demand and recharge underground aquifers.

- Plant growth can be either a burden, requiring regular upkeep, watering and chemicals, or an enhancement, providing shade and improved occupant comfort, aesthetic value, habitat for native species, and a mechanism for absorbing carbon and enriching the soil.

SUSTAINABLE SITES

SYNERGIES

The prerequisites and credits in this category work together to minimize adverse impacts to the home site. Think about the site that is being considered and evaluate how to best incorporate the home into the site.

Develop a process to integrate the following strategies: managing rainfall on the site; landscape planning that reduces need for water, fertilizers and pesticides; reducing opportunities for pests to cause damage; and, incorporating compact development strategies. All of these strategies help contribute to the health of the local and regional ecosystems.

Think about how measures in this category relate to other strategies throughout the LEED for Homes Rating System. Notice synergies such as: measures chosen in Landscaping (SS 2) should be integrated with irrigation system design (WE 2) and should be included in rainwater and graywater reuse strategies and systems (WE 1). Shading hardscape areas (SS 3) around the home can reduce irrigation needs (WE 2) as well as temper the home's outdoor environment and reduce cooling loads (EA 6), and strategies to reduce pest infestations (SS 5) are also dealt with in the development of the durability plan (ID 2.1).

THE CREDITS

SS		
SS 1: Site Stewardship	These credits require that project teams take measures prior to and during construction to limit soil erosion of surface areas surrounding the building site.
SS 2: Landscaping	These credits reward a holistic landscaping strategy that includes no invasive plants, reduced use of turf grass, and use of drought-tolerant plants.
SS 3: Local Heat Island Effects	This credit rewards projects that implement strategies to reduce the heat island effect.
SS 4: Surface Water Management	These credits reward projects that design and implement strategies to reduce stormwater runoff from the building site.
SS 5: Nontoxic Pest Control	This credit rewards homes that use one or more pest control alternatives to minimize the need for poisons.
SS 6: Compact Development	These credits reward project teams that build homes on smaller lots or increase the density of the project to reach a higher number of units per acre.

KEY TERMS

albedo	A measure of the reflectivity of a surface. High-albedo materials are very reflective of solar radiation.
borate	A wood preservative that is nontoxic to humans but highly toxic to wood-boring insects, such as termites.
buildable land	The portion of a site where construction can occur. Buildable land excludes public streets and other public rights-of-way, land occupied by nonresidential structures, public parks and land excluded from residential development by law.
built environment	The man-made alterations to a specific area, including its natural resources. On a homesite, this includes everything that has been disturbed during construction.
conventional turf	Grass, typically a monoculture, that requires considerable watering, mowing and/or fertilizers. What is considered conventional turf may vary by region.
density	The quantity of structures on a site, measured for residential buildings as dwelling units per acre of buildable land available for residential uses, and for nonresidential buildings as floor area ratio per net acre of buildable land available for nonresidential uses.
designed landscape	The arrangement of features on a site, including softscapes (such as grass and shrubs) and hardscapes (such as patios and fountains) but not areas under the roof. Preserved natural areas are not considered part of the designed landscape.
disturbed lot area	The part of a site that is directly affected by construction activity, including any activity that would compact the soil or damage vegetation.
dry well	An underground structure that collects runoff and distributes it over a large area, increasing absorption and minimizing erosion.
erosion	A process in which materials of the earth's surface are loosened, dissolved or worn away and transported by natural agents, such as water, wind or gravity.
Hardscape	Elements added to a natural landscape, such as paving stones, gravel, walkways, irrigation systems, roads, retaining walls, sculpture, street amenities, fountains, and other mechanical features. (American Society of Landscape Architects). Hardscapes are often impermeable, but they are not impermeable by definition.
invasive species	An alien species whose introduction does or is likely to cause economic or environmental harm or harm to human health. (Executive Order 13112). Not all nonnative species are considered invasive, and invasive species differ by region. Regional agencies that list invasive species are available at www.invasivespeciesinfo.gov/unitedstates/state.shtml.
local heat island effect	The incidence of higher air and surface temperatures caused by the absorption of solar energy and its reemission from roads, buildings and other structures.

mulch	A covering placed around plants to reduce erosion and water loss and to help regulate soil temperature.
native plant	A plant that has evolved within the particular habitat in which it is being used. Native plants provide food and shelter to indigenous wildlife and grow in balance with surrounding plant and animal species. The characterization of a plant as "native" may vary regionally and even locally.
no-disturbance zone	An area that is preserved during construction.
rain garden	A swale, or low tract of land into which water flows, planted with vegetation that requires or tolerates high moisture levels. A rain garden can be designed to reduce the volume of water entering storm drains and replenish groundwater.
sedimentation	The deposition of soil and other natural solids in water bodies. Sedimentation decreases water quality and accelerates the aging process of lakes, rivers and streams.
siltation	The deposition and accumulation of very fine particles in water bodies. Siltation is often harmful to lake, river and stream ecosystems.
softscape	The natural elements of a landscape, such as plant materials and soil. Softscapes can include hard elements, such as rocks.
termite	A wood-eating social insect (order Isoptera) that can cause serious structural damage to buildings in many regions of the United States. Also known as white ant.
topsoil	The uppermost layer of soil, containing high levels of nutrients and organic matter. Healthy topsoil is essential for the survival of trees and plants.
tree/plant preservation plan	A formal assessment of the lot and a development of a landscaping plan that seeks to preserve the most trees and native plants. This is important to do as one of the first steps in the design process to ensure that the developed area takes into account the preservation plan.
vegetated roof	A roof partially or fully covered by vegetation, used to manage water runoff and provide additional insulation in winter and cooling in summer.
vegetated swale	See rain garden.

PRIMARY BENEFITS

- Protects water quality.

- Prevents erosion of soils from the project site.

STANDARDS

None

INTENT

Minimize long-term environmental damage to the building lot during the construction process.

REQUIREMENTS

- Design, plan and implement appropriate erosion-control measures.

- Measures must include at a minimum the following:

  - Stockpiling and protecting disturbed topsoil from erosion (for reuse);

  - Controlling the path and velocity of runoff;

  - Protecting sewer inlets, streams and lakes;

  - Providing swales to divert surface water from hillsides; and

  - Using tiers, erosion blankets, compost blankets and the like on sloped areas.

IMPLEMENTATION

- Develop a plan for implementing erosion controls during work on the project site.

VERIFICATION & SUBMITTALS

PROJECT TEAM

- Provide erosion-control plans to the Green Rater.

GREEN RATER

- Visually verify that the required erosion-control measures have been installed.

DOCUMENTATION & CALCULATIONS

None

TIMELINE/TEAM

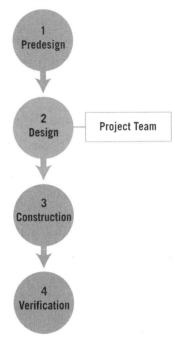

1 Predesign

2 Design — Project Team

3 Construction

4 Verification

NOTES

- Permanent erosion control measures are awarded under SS4.2.

- If the project is not fully landscaped, there must be a mechanism in place to require the homeowner to fully landscape the site within one year.

- Erosion controls and soil stabilization measures must be able to function until the landscaping is in place.

PRIMARY BENEFITS

- Prevents soil compaction.

- Protects existing trees and plants.

- Protects the natural habitat that has developed on the lot.

STANDARDS

None

INTENT

Minimize long-term environmental damage to the building lot during the construction process.

REQUIREMENTS

- Where the site is previously developed, meet either of the following conditions:

  (a) Develop a tree/plant preservation plan with no-disturbance zones; and

  (b) Leave at least 40% of the lot area undisturbed, not including area that is legally protected from disturbance and not including area under the roof of the home;

  OR

- Where the site is previously developed, meet all of the following conditions:

  (c) Develop a tree/plant preservation plan with no-disturbance zones; rehabilitate the lot, undo soil compaction and remove invasive plants; and meet the requirements of SS 2.2, Basic Landscape Design;

  OR

  (d) Build on a site that is one-seventh of an acre, or with a housing density of the project that is equal to or greater than seven units per acre.

IMPLEMENTATION

- Protect those areas of the lot that are not being used during construction.

VERIFICATION & SUBMITTALS

PROJECT TEAM

- For SS 1.2 (a) and (c) above, present a tree and plant preservation plan and/or site drawings to the Green Rater.

- For SS 1.2 (b) above, present calculations for the undisturbed area of the site to the Green Rater.

GREEN RATER

- Visually verify the tree and plant preservation plan and/or site drawings.

- Visually verify that the calculations were completed.

- Visually verify that no-disturbance zones are marked on-site.

TIMELINE/TEAM

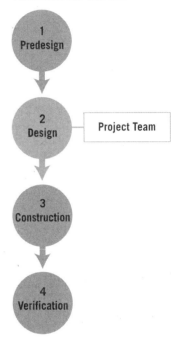

1 Predesign

2 Design — Project Team

3 Construction

4 Verification

DOCUMENTATION & CALCULATIONS

To calculate the percentage of the buildable lot area left undisturbed during construction:

1.	Take the total lot area and subtract area that is legally protected from development and subtract the area under the roof.
2.	Take the lot area that is being preserved during construction and subtract any preserved hardscapes.
3.	Divide the figure in step 2 by that in step 1 above to find the percentage of the lot area left undisturbed. This number must be at least 40%.

Sample Calculation:

Total lot = 12,500 sq ft, Legally restricted from development = 500 sq feet, Area under roof = 2,000 sq feet, Lot area preserved = 5,000 sq feet, Hardscape preserved = 750 sq feet	
Step 1:	Lot area (10,000) = 12,500 sq feet total lot – 500 sq feet not developable by local jurisdiction – 2,000 sq feet of area under roof
Step 2:	Lot area preserved (4,250) = 5,000 sq feet – 750 sq feet hardscape preserved
Step 3:	Lot area preserved (4,250 / Lot area (10,000) = 42.5% lot area left undisturbed
Project qualifies for 1 point.	

NOTES

- Undeveloped lots with substantial amounts of garbage and/or invasive weeds should be treated as previously developed sites.

- To count as previously developed, the land must have development on it that is at least 5 years old.

PRIMARY BENEFITS

- Protects native habitats and plants.

- Protects endangered species and endangered ecosystems.

STANDARDS

U.S. Executive Order 13112 defines invasive plant species.

INTENT

Design landscape features to avoid invasive species and minimize demand for water and synthetic chemicals.

REQUIREMENTS

- Introduce no invasive plant species to the landscape.

IMPLEMENTATION

- Invasive plant species vary by region. Consult the local Agricultural Cooperative Extension Service or appropriate state agency for a list of local invasive plant species.

- Select appropriate plants that do not appear on the local invasive plant species list.

VERIFICATION & SUBMITTALS

TRADE

- Provide a list of plants being used and a list of local invasive plants to the builder or project team leader.

- Sign an Accountability Form to indicate that the plants installed match those on the list provided to the builder or project team leader.

PROJECT TEAM

- Present a list of plants being used and a list of local invasive plants to the Green Rater.

- If no landscape professional is involved in the project, sign an Accountability Form to indicate that the plants that are installed match those on the lists provided to the Green Rater.

GREEN RATER

- Visually verify, using the two lists provided by the builder or project team leader, that none of the plants being used is considered invasive.

- Verify that an Accountability Form has been signed by the responsible party.

DOCUMENTATION & CALCULATIONS

None

TIMELINE/TEAM

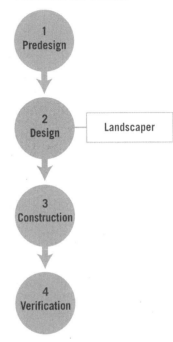

NOTES

- This measure applies to all of the designed landscape. Areas of the site that are being left alone are not required to undergo inspection.

- Areas of the site that are not being included in the landscape plan do not need to have any existing invasive plant species removed, though it is recommended.

PRIMARY BENEFITS

- Planting appropriate plants in shaded and slope areas will reduce long-term maintenance costs.

- A properly designed landscape can reduce the need for irrigation, chemicals and maintenance.

STANDARDS

None

INTENT

Design landscape features to avoid invasive species and minimize demand for water and synthetic chemicals.

REQUIREMENTS

All must be met if applicable:

- Any turf must be drought-tolerant.

- Do not use turf in densely shaded areas.

- Do not use turf in areas with a slope of 25% (4:1 slope).

- Add mulch or soil amendments as appropriate.

- All compacted soils must be tilled to at least 6 inches.

IMPLEMENTATION

- Involve the landscape professional early in the design process to ensure that all areas of the landscaping are addressed.

VERIFICATION & SUBMITTALS

TRADE

- Sign an Accountability Form to indicate that the requirements have been met.

PROJECT TEAM

- If no landscape professional is involved, sign the Accountability Form to indicate that the requirements have been met.

GREEN RATER

- Visually verify that an Accountability Form has been signed by the responsible party.

DOCUMENTATION & CALCULATIONS

None

TIMELINE/TEAM

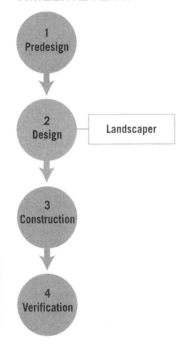

1 Predesign

2 Design — Landscaper

3 Construction

4 Verification

NOTES

- Points shown in the landscaping section of the LEED for Homes Rating System are for a fully landscaped home. A project that installs at least 50% of the landscaping will be awarded up to 50% of the landscaping points. The project team also needs to document that the remaining landscaping area will be completed within one year.

- Please note that SS 2.2, 2.3 and 2.4 can be done together or independently, but if the project team decides to use SS 2.5, SS 2.5 replaces those three measures.

PRIMARY BENEFITS

- Reduces water, fertilizer and pesticide use on lawns.

- Conventional turf typically creates a plant monoculture that reduces the ability of the soil to absorb rainwater, thus creating storm runoff and requiring significant maintenance via fertilizers, pesticides and mowing to remain healthy.

STANDARDS

None

INTENT

Design landscape features to avoid invasive species and minimize demand for water and synthetic chemicals.

REQUIREMENTS

- Limit the use of conventional turf in the designed landscape softscapes.

- Points available are based upon the percentage of landscape softscape that is conventional turf; 41–60% receives one point; 21–40% receives two points; 20% or less receives three points.

IMPLEMENTATION

- Meet early with the landscaping professional to determine the best strategy to meet the requirement.

VERIFICATION & SUBMITTALS

TRADE

- Provide calculations to the builder or project team leader.
- Sign an Accountability Form.

PROJECT TEAM

- Present calculations to the Green Rater.
- If no landscape professional is involved, sign an Accountability Form.

GREEN RATER

- Visually verify that all relevant calculations have been completed.
- Verify that an Accountability Form has been signed by the appropriate person.

DOCUMENTATION & CALCULATIONS

- Determine the total designed landscape area.
- The undisturbed portion of the lot is not to be used in this calculation.
- Estimate the total designed landscape softscape area that is planted with conventional turf.
- Calculate the percentage of the landscape that is planted with conventional turf.
- Check the points available.

TIMELINE/TEAM

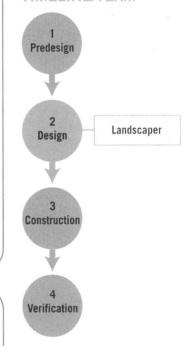

NOTES

- Please note that SS 2.2, 2.3 and 2.4 can be done together or independently, but if the project team decides to use SS 2.5, SS 2.5 replaces those three measures.

PRIMARY BENEFITS

- Reduces use of water.
- Reduces use of fertilizers.
- Reduces use of pesticides.

STANDARDS

Local drought-tolerant plant list.

INTENT

Design landscape features to avoid invasive species and minimize demand for water and synthetic chemicals.

REQUIREMENTS

- Install drought-tolerant plants.

- Points available are based upon the percentage of drought-tolerant plants in the landscape; 45–89% receives one point; 90% or more receives two points.

IMPLEMENTATION

- Meet early with the landscaping professional to determine the best strategy to meet the requirement.

VERIFICATION & SUBMITTALS

TRADE

- Provide calculations to the builder or project team leader.

- Provide a list of plants and a list of drought-tolerant plants.

- Sign an Accountability Form.

PROJECT TEAM

- Present calculations to the Green Rater.

- Present a list of plants being used and a list of plants that are drought-tolerant.

- If no landscape professional is involved, sign an Accountability Form.

GREEN RATER

- Visually verify that the calculations have been completed.

- Visually verify, using the two lists provided by the builder or project team, that any plants counted for this measure are drought-tolerant.

- Verify that an Accountability Form has been signed.

DOCUMENTATION & CALCULATIONS

- Calculate the number of drought-tolerant plants as a percentage of the total installed plants.

- Include only those plants that are newly installed, not preexisting in the landscape.

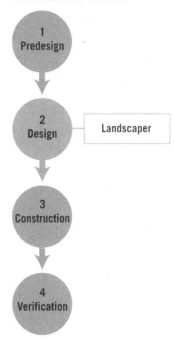

TIMELINE/TEAM

1 Predesign

2 Design — Landscaper

3 Construction

4 Verification

NOTES

- Local plants are typically drought-tolerant, reducing the need for water, fertilizers and pesticides.

- Please note that SS 2.2, 2.3 and 2.4 can be done together or independently, but if the project team decides to use SS 2.5, SS 2.5 replaces those three measures.

PRIMARY BENEFITS

- Reduces use of water.
- Reduces use of fertilizers.
- Reduces use of pesticides.

STANDARDS

None

INTENT

Design landscape features to avoid invasive species and minimize demand for water and synthetic chemicals.

REQUIREMENTS

- Design the landscape and irrigation system to reduce overall irrigation water usage.

- The estimates must be calculated and prepared by a landscape professional, biologist or other qualified professional.

- Projects can earn up to four ID points if WE2.3 has been met if the reduction in estimated irrigation water usage exceeds 65% or more:

  - 65% for one point;
  - 70% for two points;
  - 75% for three points; and
  - 80% or greater for four points.

Exemplary Performance: Projects can earn one ID point if the requirements of SS 2.2, parts b, c and d, are met.

IMPLEMENTATION

- Because of the complexity of completing this measure correctly, the involvement of a landscape professional is required. Involvement of a qualified landscape professional as early as possible is needed to ensure that all opportunities for reduction in water use are addressed.

- If a site is designed not to use any irrigation, the project team should use SS 2.5 and WE 2.3 to receive recognition for no irrigation system being installed. This process also documents that the landscaping does not need irrigation beyond the normal rainfall in the region.

VERIFICATION & SUBMITTALS

TRADE
- Provide calculations to the builder or project team leader.
- Provide a list of plants to the builder or project team leader.
- Sign an Accountability Form.
- Sign the Irrigation Calculation if used in SS.5.

PROJECT TEAM
- Present calculations to the Green Rater.
- Present a list of plants to the Green Rater.

GREEN RATER
- Visually verify that the calculations have been completed.
- Verify that an Accountability Form has been signed by the responsible party.

DOCUMENTATION & CALCULATIONS

- A calculator has been created that is embedded within the LEED for Homes Project Checklist file. Please look for the Water Use Calc tab on the LEED for Homes Checklist 2008 workbook electronic file.
- In this calculation, when calculating water use, do not subtract water from rainwater, graywater or recycled water systems.
- If no qualified professional is involved in performing this calculation, use the most conservative assumptions.
- The calculation is complex and should be performed by a qualified landscape professional, biologist or other qualified professional only. Please refer to pages 90-91 in the LEED for Homes Reference Guide, 2008, for calculation methodology.
- The calculation establishes the following, which are used to determine how well the landscape design performs:
  - Evapotranspiration rate;
  - Baseline irrigation water usage;
  - Species factor—types of plants used in the landscaping;
  - Microclimate factor—type of climate the plants will live in; and
  - Irrigation efficiency—the efficiency of the components of the irrigation equipment.
- The calculation looks at the base case for irrigation usage and compares it with the design to see how efficient the design is.

TIMELINE/TEAM

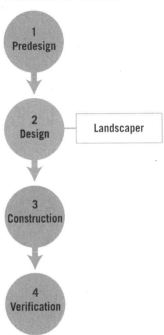

NOTES

- An integrated landscape plan reduces the need for water, fertilizers and pesticides.

- This measure, together with Water Efficiency 2.3, is a performance-based alternative to SS 2.2, 2.3 and 2.4 as well as WE 2.1 and WE 2.2. Project teams that earn points with the Performance Pathway cannot earn points for the prescriptive measures in SS 2.2, 2.3 and 2.4 or WE 2.1 and WE 2.2. The performance-based pathway provides more flexibility to reach higher reductions in irrigation use.

PRIMARY BENEFITS

- Reducing the impact of heat island effects by hardscapes reduces the need to incorporate cooling strategies in surrounding structures.

STANDARDS

None

INTENT

Design landscape features to reduce local heat island effects.

REQUIREMENTS

Do one of the following:

- Locate trees or other plantings to provide shading for at least 50% of sidewalks, patios and driveways within 50 feet of the home. Shading should be calculated for noon on June 21, when the sun is directly overhead, based on five years' growth of the plantings.

- Install light-colored, high-albedo materials or vegetation for at least 50% of sidewalks, patios and driveways within 50 feet of the home. Acceptable strategies for meeting this requirement are:

  - White concrete;
  - Gray concrete that has a solar reflectance index (SRI) of at least 29;
  - Open pavers (counting only the vegetation, not the pavers); and
  - Material with an SRI of at least 29.

- If there is no SRI rating for a product the project team can find a qualified professional to test the SRI level of the product(s).

Exemplary Performance: Projects can earn 0.5 ID point if 100% of the sidewalks, patios and driveways meet the credit requirements.

IMPLEMENTATION

- Involve a landscape professional early in the process to ensure that the plants are able to provide the necessary shading.

Exemplary Performance

VERIFICATION & SUBMITTALS

PROJECT TEAM

- Present calculations to the Green Rater.
- Sign an Accountability Form.

GREEN RATER

- Visually verify that the calculations have been completed.
- Verify that the Accountability From has been signed.

DOCUMENTATION & CALCULATIONS

Two calculation methods are acceptable:

- Percentage of Nonroof Shaded Hardscape = Shaded Area of Hardscape / Total Area of Hardscape.
- Percentage of Nonroof Light-Colored Hardscape = Light-Colored Hardscape / Total Area of Hardscape.

TIMELINE/TEAM

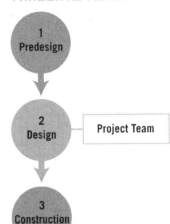

1 Predesign

2 Design — **Project Team**

3 Construction

4 Verification

NOTES

- Shading must be provided by plantings, not buildings.

PRIMARY BENEFITS

- Designing permeability into the site reduces stormwater impact, reduces the conveyance of fertilizers and pesticides to local aquifers and reduces topsoil erosion.

STANDARDS

None

INTENT

Design site features to minimize erosion and runoff from the home.

REQUIREMENTS

- Design the lot such that at least 70% of the built environment, not including area under the roof, is permeable. Areas that can be counted toward the minimum include the following:

  ○ Vegetated landscape,

  ○ Permeable paving, and

  ○ Impermeable surfaces directed to designed infiltration features.

- Points are awarded as follows for percentages of built environment that is permeable:

  ○ 70–79% = one point;

  ○ 80–89% = two points;

  ○ 90–99% = three points; and

  ○ 100% = four points.

IMPLEMENTATION

- Early in the design of the site, look for opportunities to create a permeable site through a variety of strategies that use plantings, bioswales and infiltration features for hardscape areas.

VERIFICATION & SUBMITTALS

TRADE

- Provide calculations to the builder or project team leader.
- Sign an Accountability Form.

PROJECT TEAM

- Present calculations to the Green Rater.
- If no landscaping individual is involved, sign an Accountability Form.

GREEN RATER

- Visually verify that the calculations are complete.
- Verify that the Accountability Form is signed.

DOCUMENTATION & CALCULATIONS

- Total built-environment area is total lot minus any areas that are unbuildable because of public-rights-of-way.
- Take total built-environment area and remove any area under the roof.
- Estimate the percentage of the area calculated previously that is vegetated, covered with permeable paving or designed with runoff features that qualify.

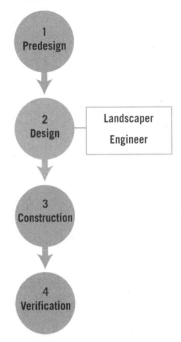

TIMELINE/TEAM

1. Predesign
2. Design — Landscaper / Engineer
3. Construction
4. Verification

NOTES

- Erosion control strategies were addressed in SS 1.1.

PRIMARY BENEFITS

- Planning and implementing erosion-control measures prevents soil erosion and protects water quality.

STANDARDS

None

INTENT

Design site features to minimize erosion and runoff from the home.

REQUIREMENTS

- Design and install one of the following:

  ○ For portions of lot on a steep slope, use terracing and retaining walls.

  ○ Plant trees, shrubs or groundcover in the following amount per 500 square feet of disturbed lot area, including area under the roof:

    - One tree (1.5-inch caliper);
    - Four 5-gallon shrubs;
    - Ten 2-gallon shrubs; and
    - 50 square feet of native groundcover.

IMPLEMENTATION

- Early in the design phase, look for opportunities to use retaining walls and terracing or plantings to reduce the opportunity for erosion.

VERIFICATION & SUBMITTALS

TRADE

- For the plants method of erosion-control, provide calculations to the builder or project team leader.

PROJECT TEAM

- For the plants method of erosion control, present calculations to the Green Rater.

GREEN RATER

- For the plants method of erosion control, visually verify that the calculations have been completed.

- Visually verify that the appropriate measures have been installed.

DOCUMENTATION & CALCULATIONS

- Trees Required = Total Disturbed Lot Area / 500 Square Feet.

  OR

- Shrubs Required = (Total Disturbed Area / 500 Square Feet) X 4.

  OR

- Native Groundcover Plants Required = 10% X Total Disturbed Lot Area.

TIMELINE/TEAM

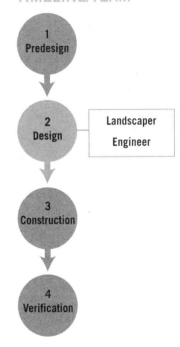

1 Predesign

2 Design — Landscaper / Engineer

3 Construction

4 Verification

NOTES

- Total disturbed area is the amount of land that is disturbed by construction of the home. This includes the area under the roof of the home.

PRIMARY BENEFITS

- Managing the rainfall that is collected from the roof reduces the impact of stormwater runoff that can harm the surrounding environment.

STANDARDS

None

INTENT

Design site features to minimize erosion and runoff from the home.

REQUIREMENTS

- Design and install one or more of the following runoff-control measures:

  ○ Install a vegetated roof to cover 50% of the roof (0.5 point);

  ○ Install a vegetated roof to cover 100% of the roof (1 point);

  ○ Install permanent stormwater controls to manage runoff from the roof (1 point); and

  ○ Have the lot designed by a professional to manage runoff from the home on-site (2 points).

IMPLEMENTATION

- Investigate options for retaining rainwater that falls on the roof through a variety of strategies.

- Incorporate strategies that slow the flow of stormwater to allow the water to filter locally and recharge the local aquifer.

VERIFICATION & SUBMITTALS

TRADE

- For measure SS4.3 (d),the professional that is responsible for the measure must sign an Accountability Form.

PROJECT TEAM

- Present calculations to the Green Rater.

- Present the Accountability Form to the Green Rater.

GREEN RATER

- Visually verify that the relevant measures have been installed.

- Verify that an Accountability Form has been signed by the professional responsible for designing and implementing SS 4.3 (d).

DOCUMENTATION & CALCULATIONS

- Calculate the amount of roof that is covered by vegetation.

TIMELINE/TEAM

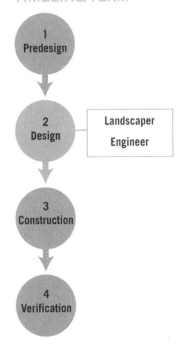

NOTES

- SS 4.3 (d) requires that a licensed or certified landscape professional or engineering professional design the site to manage the rainwater on-site.

PRIMARY BENEFITS

- Improves durability of the home.

INTENT

Design home features to minimize the need for poisons to control insects, rodents and other pests.

STANDARDS

2000 International Residential Building Code™

REQUIREMENTS

- Implement one or more of the following measures (0.5 point each, for a maximum of 2 points):

  ○ Available for use in all regions of the country:

    - Keep all wood at least 12 inches above the soil (internal framing that is separated from soil or air by foundation walls does not need to comply, nor do porches or decks).
    - Seal all cracks, joints and so on with caulking, and install pest-proof screens.
    - Include no wood-to-concrete connections, or separate them with dividers.
    - Install landscaping so that mature plants are 24 feet from the home.

  ○ In areas of "moderate" to "very heavy" termite risk, as defined by the 2000 International Residential Building Code™, implement one or more of the following measures (0.5 point each):

    - Treat all cellulosic material with borate product to 3 feet above the foundation;
    - Install sand or a diatomaceous earth barrier;
    - Install a steel-mesh barrier termite-control system;
    - Install a nontoxic termite bait system;
    - Use noncellulosic wall structures; and
    - Use solid concrete foundation walls or a pest-proof masonry wall design.

Exemplary Performance: Each additional measure incorporated beyond the maximum four measures is awarded at 0.5 point per measure, for a maximum of 1.0 ID point.

IMPLEMENTATION

- A risk assessment is the first step in determining the necessary steps to control insect infestation. Once this has been done, select the appropriate measures to minimize the risk.

VERIFICATION & SUBMITTALS

GREEN RATER

- Visually verify that all relevant measures are complete.

DOCUMENTATION & CALCULATIONS

None

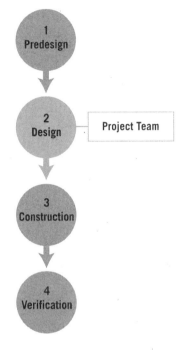

TIMELINE/TEAM

1 Predesign

2 Design — Project Team

3 Construction

4 Verification

NOTES

- Address strategies and measures that reduce the impact of pests, such as termites, improve the durability of the home.

PRIMARY BENEFITS

- Building compact developments uses available land efficiently and protects habitat from development.

STANDARDS

None

INTENT

Make use of compact development patterns to conserve land and promote community livability, transportation efficiency and walkability.

REQUIREMENTS

Measure	Housing Density
6.1: Moderate Density (2 Points)	Average housing density of one-seventh of an acre. One home on one-seventh acre qualifies.
6.2: High Density (3 Points)	Average housing density of one-tenth of an acre. One home on one-tenth acre qualifies.
6.3: Very High Density (4 Points)	Average housing density of one-twentieth of an acre. One home on one-twentieth acre qualifies.

Exemplary Performance: Projects with a density greater than 40 dwelling units per acre may submit a request for an exemplary performance point through their LEED for Homes Provider.

IMPLEMENTATION

- Look for opportunities to build smaller homes on smaller lots.

VERIFICATION & SUBMITTALS

PROJECT TEAM

- Present calculations to the Green Rater.

GREEN RATER

- Visually verify the housing density calculations.

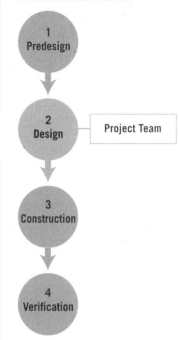

1 Predesign

2 Design — Project Team

3 Construction

4 Verification

DOCUMENTATION & CALCULATIONS

- Average Density = Number of Housing Units / Acres of Buildable Land.

- Buildable land area is calculated as follows:

  - Exclude public streets or public rights-of-way, land occupied by nonresidential structures, public parks, and land excluded from residential development by law.

  - For multiple-lot developments, include only the sum of the lot areas for homes being built for LEED for Homes.

  - The numerator is the number of housing units in the project; the denominator, the buildable land area included in the project (subject to the above exclusions). Both relate to the project only, not the surrounding area.

NOTES

- SS 1.2 is automatically granted to moderate, high, or very-high density homes.

1   What are strategies for reducing the need for irrigation on a home site?

_____

_____

2   What are strategies for reducing the need for pesticides on a home site?

_____

_____

3   Make a list of strategies that reduce the heat island effect of the home and site.

_____

_____

4   What are strategies for managing rainwater runoff from the home and site?

_____

_____

Conduct an informational interview with a green land-scape professional to learn about best practices alter-natives to conventional turf for homes in your area.

ASK AROUND

Observe erosion control measures on a residential site under construction for a conventional home. Note which strategies are being used and which are not. Comment on the effectiveness of the strategies being used. (If time allows, make the same observations and notes for a home that is being built using the LEED for Homes Rating System).

SITE VISIT

Make a list of all of the invasive plant species in your region. Use the resources available from the U.S. Department of Agriculture at

http://www.invasivespeciesinfo.gov/council/main.shtml

1.	
2.	
3.	
4.	
5.	
6.	

INVESTIGATE

1 Construction can contribute to site disturbance by (Select Two.)

A) killing trees and shrubs.

B) increasing noise levels.

C) emitting particulates into the air.

D) displacing wildlife.

2 During a review of the site, you discover several invasive plant species. What is required of the project team?

A) You only need to remove plants on the noxious weed list.

B) You need to remove all invasive plant species from the entire site.

C) Invasive plant species that are found outside of the landscape plan area do not need to be removed from the site.

D) Invasive plant species can be left on the site with approval from a landscape professional.

3 Shading hardscapes around the home is a process that is intended to ___?

A) minimize soil compaction.

B) improve stormwater management.

C) reduce local heat island effects.

D) minimize paved areas.

4 According to SS 4, Surface Water Management, what are some of the strategies for improving the permeability of the lot? (Select Two).

A) A driveway that drains into the municipal stormwater system.

B) A mixed landscape of native plants and drought-tolerant grass.

C) A 1400 Sq. Ft. 1-story home on a 2000 Sq. Ft. lot.

D) A 1400 Sq. Ft. 2-story home on a 2000 Sq. Ft. lot.

E) A vegetated roof covering 100% of the roof area.

5 In the Sustainable Sites 2.5 measure, a home that reduces overall irrigation demand by more than 45% is eligible to ___?

A) apply for a National Pollutant Discharge Elimination System (NPDES) award.

B) be counted in the calculation for points in Water Efficiency 1.1, 1.2 and 1.3 credits.

C) also earn points under the Water Efficiency 2.3 credit.

D) be a WaterSense program demonstration site.

See Answer Key on page 267.

WATER EFFICIENCY

The Water Efficiency (WE) category addresses environmental concerns relating to water use and disposal. Discharged water contaminates rivers, lakes and potable water with bacteria, nitrogen, toxic metals and other contaminants. Each credit encourages the use of strategies and technologies that reduce the amount of potable water consumed.

WHAT ABOUT WATER EFFICIENCY?

How does water leave your site, where does it go?

How much water is used to maintain conventional landscaping? Are there low-water alternatives?

Why are approximately one-third of the nation's lakes, stream and rivers unsafe for swimming and fishing?

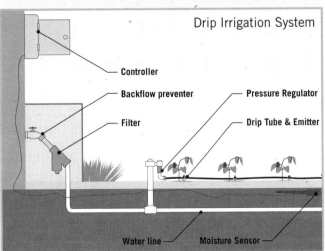

Drip Irrigation System

Controller

Backflow preventer

Pressure Regulator

Filter

Drip Tube & Emitter

Water line

Moisture Sensor

WATER EFFICIENCY

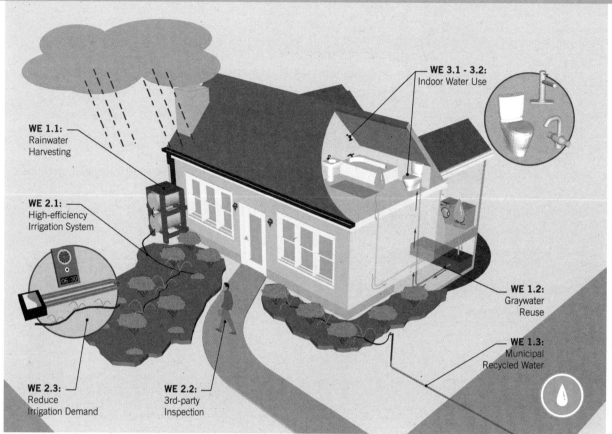

WE 3.1 - 3.2:
Indoor Water Use

WE 1.1:
Rainwater
Harvesting

WE 2.1:
High-efficiency
Irrigation System

WE 1.2:
Graywater
Reuse

WE 1.3:
Municipal
Recycled Water

WE 2.3:
Reduce
Irrigation Demand

WE 2.2:
3rd-party
Inspection

THE OVERVIEW

Water efficiency measures in new homes can easily reduce water usage by 30% or more. In a typical home, savings of 30,000 gallons of water a year can be achieved very cost-effectively. This results in average annual water utility savings of about $100 per year.

As communities grow, increased demand for water leads to additional maintenance and higher costs for municipal supply and treatment facilities. New homes that use water efficiently have lower water use fees and reduced sewage volumes. Many water conservation strategies involve either no additional cost or short-term paybacks, whereas other strategies, such as rainwater harvesting and graywater plumbing systems, often involve more substantial investment.

WATER EFFICIENCY

SYNERGIES

The credits in this section address two main areas of water use, outdoor and indoor applications. Think about how water arrives at the home site, how it is used and finally how it is discharged. This holistic, full-cycle approach to reusing water can reduce the demand for potable water and the amount of water that needs to be discharged from the site. The key is to capture the water that arrives on the site and apply efficient outdoor and indoor applications for the site.

Rainwater capturing can provide for landscape irrigation or use inside the home for flushing the toilet, washing clothes, and other purposes. Graywater capture strategies can also use indoor waste water for toilet flushing and landscape water use.

These strategies that incorporate landscape that has been designed to use rainwater or graywater integrate a holistic approach to water use. Indoor applications that use water-efficient fixtures help complete the cycle by using less water. Creating an integrated system that uses the natural water cycle reduces water needs at the home site.

Rainwater harvesting and graywater reuse irrigation systems (WE 1) should be integrated with resource-efficient landscape (SS 2) and irrigation system design (WE 2). Think about how basic landscape design and landscape irrigation demand impact these measures. Also, using water uses energy. Points for indoor water distribution-related savings are available under Efficient Hot Water Distribution Systems (EA 7.1); and points for appliance related water savings are available under Appliances (EA 9).

THE CREDITS

WE 1: Water Reuse	These credits reward project teams that implement strategies to use site captured water, either from rainwater, graywater or municipal recycled water systems.
WE 2: Irrigation Systems	These credits reward project teams that design and incorporate strategies that implement either a water-efficient irrigation system or a landscaping that does not need an irrigation system.
WE 3: Indoor Water Use	These credits reward the installation of either high-efficiency or very high-efficiency fixtures in bathrooms.

KEY TERMS

catchment	The surface area of a roof that captures rainwater for a rainwater harvesting system.
compensating shower valves	Designed to keep bathing water temperatures in the shower fairly constant when other appliances, such as a washing machine or toilet, are in use and when the hot or cold water supply pressures change or the bathing water outlet temperature changes. Three types of valves are available: Thermostatic compensating valves are designed to keep bathing water temperatures in the shower fairly constant when other appliances, such as a washing machine or toilet, are in use and when the hot or cold water supply pressures change or the bathing water outlet temperature changes. The response of this type of mechanism differs from that of a pressure balance compensating valve. Pressure balance compensating valves are designed to keep bathing water temperature in the shower fairly constant when other appliances, such as a washing machine or toilet, are in use and when the hot or cold water supply pressures change. Conventional, noncompensating valves are completely dependent on the user to adjust the temperature at all times.
demand-controlled circulation	The automatic circulation of water, triggered by a switch or sensor, through a looped system to ensure that hot water is immediately available while keeping unused cold water in the system, saving both water and energy.
distribution uniformity	A metric for estimating how uniformly water is applied to an area. Distribution uniformity (DU) ranges between 0 and 1, where 1 indicates that the irrigation system is providing perfectly equal coverage. A higher DU means less likelihood of overwatering or underwatering.
drip irrigation system	A network of pipes and valves that rest on the soil or underground and slowly deliver water to the root systems of plants. Drip irrigation saves water by minimizing evapotranspiration and topsoil runoff. Drip irrigation usually involves a network of pipes and valves that rest on the soil or underground at the root zone.
dual-flush toilet	A toilet with two flush volumes, one for solid waste and a reduced volume for liquid waste.
graywater	Wastewater that comes from household baths and clothes washers and is neither clean nor heavily soiled. More specifically: (1) "Untreated house-hold wastewater which has not come into contact with toilet waste. Graywater includes used water from bathtubs, showers, bathroom wash basins, and water from clothes-washers and laundry tubs. It shall not include wastewater from kitchen sinks or dishwashers" (Uniform Plumbing Code, Appendix G, "Grey Water Systems for Single-Family Dwellings"). (2) "Wastewater discharged from lavatories, bathtubs, showers, clothes washers, and laundry sinks" (International Plumbing Code, Appendix C, "Grey Water Recycling Systems"). Some states and local authorities allow kitchen sink wastewater to be included in graywater.

WATER EFFICIENCY KEY TERMS

high-efficiency toilet (HET)	A toilet that uses no more than 1.3 gallons per flush.
potable	Suitable for drinking. Potable water is generally supplied by municipal water systems.

PRIMARY BENEFITS

- Reduces use of potable water for irrigation and toilet flushing.

STANDARDS

None

INTENT

Use municipal recycled water or offset central water supply through the capture and controlled reuse of rainwater and/or graywater.

REQUIREMENTS

- Design and install a rainwater harvesting and storage system for landscaping irrigation and/or indoor water use.

- Follow the calculation method below.

  - For indoor use, minimum storage tank capacity: 50% of the roof area (two points).

  - For outdoor use, minimum storage capacity: 50% of the roof area (three points).

  - For indoor/outdoor use, minimum storage capacity: 75% of the roof area (four points).

Exemplary Performance: Projects that install a system sized to capture rainwater from 100% of the roof area and can demonstrate a demand for this water can apply for one additional point, to be counted under ID 3, Innovative or Regional Design. This application must be submitted to the LEED for Homes Provider and approved by USGBC before the point can be awarded.

IMPLEMENTATION

- Proper sizing of the system is the key to homeowner satisfaction and use. For the system to work adequately, efficient irrigation and indoor water use products should be as efficient as possible.

- The rainwater harvesting system can be used to capture rainwater to irrigate the landscape and/or for indoor applications. Sizing the system for outdoor use will vary by region, though the criteria the system uses are the same throughout the country.

- Storage system tanks should be opaque, kept out of direct sunlight and kept covered to keep out debris.

VERIFICATION & SUBMITTALS

PROJECT TEAM

- Present calculations to the Green Rater.

- Include any rainwater harvesting system equipment literature in the occupant's operation and maintenance manual.

GREEN RATER

- Visually verify that all calculations related to this credit are completed.

- Visually verify that the rainwater harvesting system has been installed.

DOCUMENTATION & CALCULATIONS

- Determine the rainwater harvest system size area as a percentage of the total area of the roof:

  ○ System Size (percentage) = Harvest Area / Total Roof Area.

- Determine the minimum storage capacity:

  ○ Storage Capacity Required = 0.62 Gallon/per Square Foot X Harvest Area.

  ○ One square foot with 1 inch of rain equals 0.62 gallon of water.

TIMELINE/TEAM

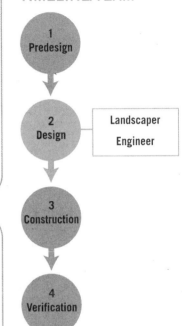

NOTES

- A home using a municipal recycled water system cannot receive points under WE 1.1 or WE 1.2 for outdoor applications.

PRIMARY BENEFITS

- Using potable water resources more than once reduces the impact of home water use on water resources.

STANDARDS

Uniform Plumbing Code

INTENT

Use municipal recycled water or offset central water supply through the capture and controlled reuse of rainwater and/or graywater.

REQUIREMENTS

- Design and install a graywater reuse system for landscape irrigation use or indoor water use.

- Septic systems do not qualify.

- The system must include a tank or dosing basin that can be used as part of the irrigation system.

- Graywater must be collected from one or more of the following sources:

  - Clothes washer;

  - Showers; and

  - Some combination of faucets and other sources estimated to exceed 5,000 gallons per year.

Exemplary Performance: Projects that install a graywater system that collects water from multiple sources such as washers, showers or wash basins and can demonstrate a demand for this water can apply for one additional point, to be counted under ID 3, Innovative or Regional Design.

IMPLEMENTATION

- A graywater reuse system needs to be designed by a licensed plumber and must meet all applicable local codes.

VERIFICATION & SUBMITTALS

PROJECT TEAM

- Present calculations for the graywater reuse system and surge tank size to the Green Rater.

- Include any system equipment information in the occupant's operations and maintenance manual.

GREEN RATER

- Visually verify that all calculations related to this credit are completed.

- Visually verify that the graywater reuse system has been installed.

DOCUMENTATION & CALCULATIONS

- Determine the amount of water generated from faucets and other uses if pursuing the 5,000 gallons or more qualification pathway.

TIMELINE/TEAM

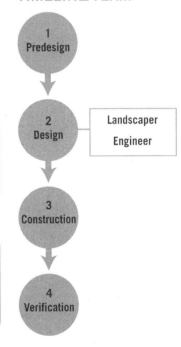

1 Predesign

2 Design — Landscaper / Engineer

3 Construction

4 Verification

NOTES

- Graywater is defined under the Uniform Plumbing Code as "untreated household wastewater which has not come into contact with toilet waste."

- Local codes may restrict or not allow the use of graywater.

- A home using a municipal recycled water system cannot receive points under WE 1.1 or WE 1.2 for outdoor applications.

- The piping used for this strategy is usually purple.

PRIMARY BENEFITS

- Using potable water resources more than once reduces the impact on water resources.

STANDARDS

None

INTENT

Use municipal recycled water or offset central water supply through the capture and controlled reuse of rainwater and/or graywater.

REQUIREMENTS

- Design the plumbing such that irrigation system water demand is supplied by municipal recycled water.

- This measure is only applicable to those communities that have a municipal recycled water program.

IMPLEMENTATION

- Investigate options for using a municipal recycled water program when the home is under conceptual or schematic design.

- Implementation of this strategy will require that a second set of pipes be installed at the homesite. They will be marked as a nonpotable water source.

VERIFICATION & SUBMITTALS

PROJECT TEAM

- Provide evidence from the municipal recycled water system that the system is in place.

- Include any system equipment information in the occupant's operations and maintenance manual.

GREEN RATER

- Visually verify that the home is plumbed to receive recycled water from a municipal recycled water system.

DOCUMENTATION & CALCULATIONS

None

TIMELINE/TEAM

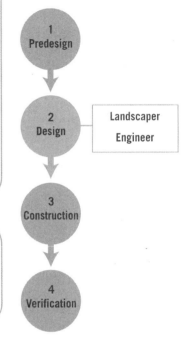

NOTES

- A municipal recycled water system takes potable water that has been used once and cleans it (though not to potable water standards) and sends it back to homeowners and buildings for landscape use.

- The piping used for this strategy is usually purple.

- A home using a municipal recycled water system cannot receive points under WE 1.1 or WE 1.2 for outdoor applications.

PRIMARY BENEFITS

- A high-efficiency irrigation system will reduce the use of water to the level that is appropriate for the planted landscape.

STANDARDS

None

INTENT

Minimize outdoor demand for water through water-efficient irrigation.

REQUIREMENTS

- Install a high-efficiency irrigation system or device from the following list. For full details, see page 145 of the LEED for Homes Reference Guide, 2008. (one point each, up to three points total):

  - Irrigation system designed by EPA Water Sense certified professional.
  - Irrigation system with head-to-head coverage.
  - Central shut-off valve.
  - Submeter for irrigation system.
  - Drip irrigation for 50% of planting beds.
  - Separate zones for each type of bedding.
  - Timer of controller for each watering zone.
  - Pressure-regulating devices.
  - High-efficiency nozzles with distribution uniformity of at least 0.70.
  - Check valves in heads.
  - Moisture sensor or rain delay controller.

Exemplary Performance: Projects that implement irrigation measures beyond the maximum 3 points can earn points to be counted under ID 3. Each measure is worth 0.5 point, with a maximum of 2 exemplary performance points awarded.

IMPLEMENTATION

- Use a landscape professional to select and install the correct type of irrigation system:

  1. Ascertain the goals of the homeowner to determine the types of landscaping that can be planted.

  2. Determine the watering needs of the landscaping, grouping similar water-need plants together.

  3. Select an irrigation system that will meet the needs of the landscaping.

VERIFICATION & SUBMITTALS

TRADE

- Sign an Accountability Form to indicate that the installed system meets the requirements of the credit.

- Deliver any equipment literature (such as user manuals, brochures and specifications) to the builder or project team leader.

PROJECT TEAM

- Include any system equipment information in the occupant's operations and maintenance manual.

GREEN RATER

- Verify that an Accountability Form has been signed by the responsible party.

- Where appropriate, visually verify that all applicable elements of the irrigation system, such as controls, sensors and meters, are installed.

DOCUMENTATION & CALCULATIONS

None

TIMELINE/TEAM

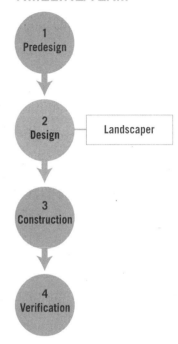

NOTES

- Points shown in the landscaping section of the LEED for Homes Rating System are for a fully landscaped home. A project that installs at least 50% of the landscaping will be awarded up to 50% of the landscaping points. The project team also needs to document that the remaining landscaping area will be completed within one year.

- If a site is designed not to use any irrigation, the project team should use SS 2.5 and WE 2.3 to receive recognition for no irrigation system being installed. This process also documents that the landscaping does not need irrigation beyond the normal rainfall in the region.

- Project teams pursing WE 2.1 and/or WE 2.2 cannot receive points for WE 2.3.

PRIMARY BENEFITS

- Third-party verification of the proper functioning of the irrigation system helps ensure that the system is working as designed.

STANDARDS

None

INTENT

Minimize outdoor demand for water through water-efficient irrigation.

REQUIREMENTS

- Have a third party inspect the irrigation system to observe the following:
  - Spray heads are operating and delivering water to intended zones;
  - All switches or shutoff valves are set properly;
  - Any timers or controllers are set properly;
  - Any irrigation systems are located at least 2 feet from the home; and
  - Irrigation spray does not hit the home.

IMPLEMENTATION

- Involve the third-party verifier early in the irrigation system installation process to ensure that the measures can be verified.

VERIFICATION & SUBMITTALS

PROJECT TEAM

- Include any system equipment information in the occupant's operations and maintenance manual.

GREEN RATER

- Verify that an Accountability Form has been signed by the responsible party.

- Where appropriate, visually verify that all applicable elements of the irrigation system, such as controls, sensors and meters, are installed.

DOCUMENTATION & CALCULATIONS

None

TIMELINE/TEAM

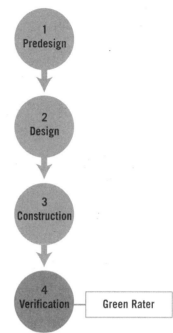

NOTES

- Project teams pursing WE 2.1 and/or WE 2.2 cannot receive points for WE 2.3.

PRIMARY BENEFITS

- This measure, together with Sustainable Sites 2.5, is a performance-based alternative to SS 2.2, 2.3 and 2.4 as well as WE 2.1 and WE 2.2. Project teams that earn points with the Performance Pathway cannot earn points for the prescriptive measures in SS 2.2, 2.3 and 2.4 or WE 2.1 and WE 2.2. The performance-based pathway provides more flexibility to reach higher reductions in irrigation use.

STANDARDS

None

INTENT

Minimize outdoor demand for water through water-efficient irrigation.

REQUIREMENTS

- Design the landscape and irrigation system to reduce overall irrigation water usage.

- The estimates must be calculated and prepared by a landscape professional, biologist or other qualified professional.

Table 1 from the LEED for Homes Reference Guide, 2008. Page 146. Reduction in Water Demand.

Reduction in estimated irrigation water usage	WE 2.3 points	SS 2.5 points	Total points
45–49%	1	6	7
45–49%	2	6	8
55–59%	3	6	9
60% or more	4	6	10

- Projects can earn up to four ID points if the reduction in estimated irrigation water usage exceeds 65% or more:
  - 65% for one point;
  - 70% for two points;
  - 75% for three points; and
  - 80% or greater for four points.

Exemplary Performance: Projects can earn one ID point if the requirements of SS 2.2, parts b, c and d, are met.

IMPLEMENTATION

- Because of the complexity of completing this measure correctly, the involvement of a landscape professional is required. Involvement of a qualified landscape professional as early as possible is needed to ensure that all opportunities for reduction in water use are addressed.

- The LEED for Homes program has developed an irrigation calculator that automates the irrigation calculation. It is recommended, though not required, that the landscape professional use the irrigation calculator.

VERIFICATION & SUBMITTALS

TRADE
- Provide calculations to the builder or project team leader.
- Provide a list of plants to the builder or project team leader.
- Sign an Accountability Form.

PROJECT TEAM
- Present calculations to the Green Rater.
- Present a list of plants to the Green Rater.

GREEN RATER
- Visually verify that the calculations have been completed.
- Verify that an Accountability Form has been signed by the responsible party.

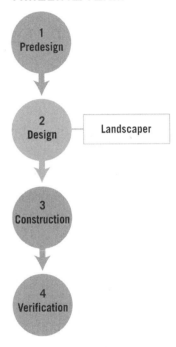

TIMELINE/TEAM

1 Predesign

2 Design — Landscaper

3 Construction

4 Verification

DOCUMENTATION & CALCULATIONS

- In this calculation, when calculating water use, do not subtract water from rainwater, graywater or recycled water systems.
- If no qualified professional is involved in performing this calculation, use the most conservative assumptions.
- The calculation is complex and should be performed by a qualified landscape professional, biologist or other qualified professional. Please refer to pages 146-147 in the LEED for Homes Reference Guide, 2008, for calculation methodology.
- The calculation establishes the following, which are used to determine how well the landscape design performs:
  - Evapotranspiration rate;
  - Baseline irrigation water usage;
  - Species factor: the types of plants used in the landscaping;
  - Microclimate factor: the type of climate the plants will live in; and
  - Irrigation efficiency: the efficiency of the components of the irrigation equipment.
- The calculation looks at the base case for irrigation usage and compares it with the design to see how efficient the design is.
- A calculator has been created that is embedded within the LEED for Homes Project Checklist file. Please look for the Water Use Calculation tab on the LEED for Homes Checklist 2008 workbook electronic file.

NOTES

- Designing a water-efficient landscape is the first step. The second step is ensuring that only the proper amount of water is provided to maintain that landscape.

PRIMARY BENEFITS

- Indoor water-efficient fixtures reduce water use.

STANDARDS

ASME A112.19.14

WaterSense

INTENT

Minimize indoor demand for water through water-efficient fixtures and fittings.

REQUIREMENTS

WE 3.1: (1 point each, maximum of 3 points):
- The average flow rate of all lavatory faucets must be ≤ 2.0 gpm.
- The average flow rate of all showers must be ≤ 2.0 gpm.
- The average flow rate of all toilets must be ≤ 1.3 gpf.
  - Toilets must be dual-flush and meet ASME Standard A112.19.14.
    OR
  - Toilets must meet U.S. EPA WaterSense specifications and be certified and labeled accordingly.

WE 3.2: (2 points each, maximum of 6 points):
- The average flow rate of all lavatory faucets must be ≤ 1.5 gpm.
  - Faucets must meet U.S. EPA WaterSense specifications and be certified and labeled accordingly.
- The average flow rate of all showers must be ≤ 1.75 gpm.
- The average flow rate of all toilets must be ≤ 1.1 gpf.

Exemplary Performance: Projects that can demonstrate flow rates that are significantly lower than those in WE 3.2 can earn one additional point in ID. This request must be submitted to the LEED for Homes Provider and approved by USGBC before the point can be counted.

IMPLEMENTATION

- Select the most efficient indoor fixtures with which the homeowner is comfortable. Studies have shown that there is a high frustration level if showerhead flow, faucet flow and toilet flushing do not perform as expected. Ensure that the products selected have a high satisfaction level on any consumer rating website.

IMPLEMENTATION, CONTINUED

- Kitchen, laundry and mudroom fixtures are exempt from this measure.

- Compensating shower valves and conventional, noncompensating shower valves may not work properly when low-flow showerheads (those that restrict water flow below 2.5 gpm) are installed. Make sure any low-flow showerhead is installed with a valve that has been designed, tested and verified to function safely at the reduced flow rate. If in doubt, consult the manufacturer of the valve before installing a low-flow showerhead.

VERIFICATION & SUBMITTALS

PROJECT TEAM

- Include any equipment literature in the occupant's operations and maintenance manual.

GREEN RATER

- Visually verify that all fixtures and fittings meet the appropriate requirements.

DOCUMENTATION & CALCULATIONS

- All fixtures need to meet the requirements for the points to be awarded. An averaging protocol is available and is shown in the "calculation overview" section.

- The total water usage per shower must be less than or equal to 3 gpm. Multiple showerheads in one shower cannot simply average the showerhead rate.

- Toilets calculation:
  - Average Volume = [(High Volume Flush) + 2 X (Low Volume Flush)] / 3.

- Overall average efficiency of each fixture:
  - Two lavatory faucets flow at a rate of 1.5 gpm and a third flows at a rate of 2.1 gpm: Average Efficiency = (1.5 + 1.5 + 2.1) / 3 = 1.7 gallons.

TIMELINE/TEAM

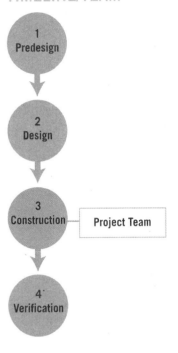

NOTES

- The project cannot earn points in WE 3.1 and WE 3.2 for the same fixture.

1 Name and define three types of water in relation to water reuse.

_____

_____

2 What are the 11 potential factors that qualify an irrigation system as high efficiency under WE 2?

_____

_____

3 What environmental issues pertaining to graywater must be considered and what steps can you take to address these issues?

_____

_____

4 Graywater systems must meet state and local health codes and standards. Research, compare and contrast standards for your area and two other U.S. cities.

_____

_____

SITE VISIT

Visit a home improvement store to look at high-efficiency fixtures and residential irrigation systems. Read the product literature and look for gpm and gpf ratings.

A) Make a list of all the products with an EPA WaterSense label.

B) Make a list of some products that are otherwise described as high-efficiency.

C) Locate the moisture sensor controllers and rain delay controllers.

ASK AROUND

Conduct an informational interview with an employee of your local water bureau to find out what rebates or incentives are available for homeowners and home builders.

INVESTIGATE

Visit EPA's website pertaining to WaterSense at

www.epa.gov/owm/water efficiency/pp/irrprof.htm

WE PRACTICE QUESTIONS

1 Your project team is looking at incorporating water harvesting strategies for the project. Which scenario would earn them the most points?

A) Rainwater harvesting from 50% or more of the roof area for indoor and outdoor applications

B) Rainwater harvesting from 50% or more of the roof area for outdoor applications

C) Rainwater harvesting from 75% or more of the roof area for indoor applications

D) Rainwater harvesting from 75% or more of the roof area for indoor and outdoor applications

2 If the builder incorporates landscaping measures from the approved list, but only does so in the front yard, what is the outcome?

A) Points can only be awarded by a Green Rater or the Provider.

B) No points may be earned.

C) Half of the points may be earned.

D) All points may be earned.

3 Which of the following qualifies for the highest performance level with regard to Very High Efficiency Fixtures and Fittings?

A) A dual-flush toilet with the U.S. EPA WaterSense label

B) A toilet with an average flow rate that is 1.2 gpf or more

C) A lavatory faucet with an average flow rate of 2.0 gpm or more

D) A shower with an average flow rate of 1.5 gpm or less

4 Your project is eligible to earn points for the Sustainable Sites 2.5, Reduce Overall Irrigation, measure. Now that you've chosen this pathway, additional points for irrigation system improvements may only be earned by ___?

A) Rezoning the irrigation system to deliver less water to different plantings.

B) Having a third-party inspector verify the site.

C) Incorporating the Water Efficiency 2.3 measure.

D) Utilizing high-efficiency nozzles with an average DU of 0.20.

5 The team has installed an irrigation system and plans to have a third-party inspector verify the system. Which of the following must the third-party inspector observe in accordance with Water Efficiency 2.2? (Select Two.)

A) Any irrigation system must be located at least 18 inches from the home.

B) All switches or shut-off valves are working properly.

C) The irrigation spray does not hit the home.

D) A 45% reduction in irrigation water usage.

E) 45% of all landscaped plants are drought tolerant.

See Answer Key on page 268.

ENERGY & ATMOSPHERE

The Energy & Atmosphere (EA) category addresses energy consumption and demand issues by encouraging the use of strategies and technologies that reduce the amount of energy consumed and promote the use of new, clean, alternative energy sources.

WHAT ABOUT ENERGY & ATMOSPHERE?

- How has the average home size in the U.S. changed over the past 50 years? How does this impact fossil fuel use?

- How much energy does the average American use? How does this compare to an average person in China or India?

- How does coal-fired electricity generation impact human health?

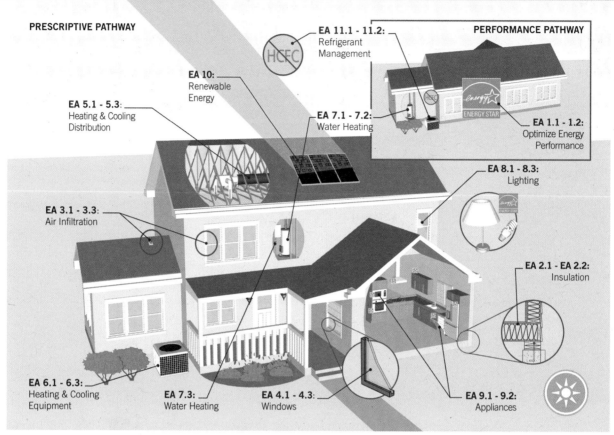

PRESCRIPTIVE PATHWAY

EA 11.1 - 11.2:
Refrigerant
Management

PERFORMANCE PATHWAY

EA 10:
Renewable
Energy

EA 5.1 - 5.3:
Heating & Cooling
Distribution

EA 7.1 - 7.2:
Water Heating

EA 1.1 - 1.2:
Optimize Energy
Performance

EA 8.1 - 8.3:
Lighting

EA 3.1 - 3.3:
Air Infiltration

EA 2.1 - EA 2.2:
Insulation

EA 6.1 - 6.3:
Heating & Cooling
Equipment

EA 7.3:
Water Heating

EA 4.1 - 4.3:
Windows

EA 9.1 - 9.2:
Appliances

THE OVERVIEW

Building green homes is one of the best strategies for meeting the challenge of climate change because the technology to substantially reduce energy and carbon dioxide (CO_2) emissions already exists. The average LEED-certified home uses 30% to 40% less electricity and saves more than 100 metric tons of CO_2 emissions over its lifetime.

The average mix of end uses of energy in U.S. homes is summarized in Figure 1. The actual percentages vary with climate and location: Homes in the North use proportionally more energy for space heating and less for electric air-conditioning than homes in the South, and vice versa, but these uses nevertheless represent the primary target areas for energy efficiency improvements.

Creating a holistic energy performance path for homes requires incorporating strategies, materials and equipment that work together to deliver the same comfort while using less energy.

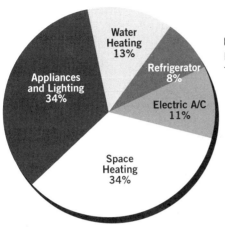

Figure 1 from the LEED for Homes Reference Guide, 2008. Page 166.
Energy Use in U.S. Homes. (Source: 2005 Building Energy Data Book, Table 4.2.1)

SYNERGIES

The prerequisites and credits in this category incorporate strategies and measures that impact energy performance of the home. Think about how potential energy arrives at the site, how it is used, how it can be used more efficiently, and how it can be monitored to impact how energy use can be modified by the occupant of the home.

Develop processes that incorporate energy reducing strategies into the home building process. These strategies will need to look at the home as a whole. This provides several distinct steps. It starts with looking at how the design of the home impacts energy use, and then moves onto field implementation of that design in the construction techniques applied to the home. Then, investigating mechanical equipment use and installation ensures that they are appropriate for the design and installed properly.

Whether you choose to utilize renewable energy strategies or install efficient systems into the home, the measures in this category relate to a number of other strategies throughout the LEED for Homes Rating System. For example, HVAC and framing efficiency are closely linked; floor, ceiling, and roof framing layouts should be designed to use framing material efficiently and at the same time accommodate duct runs as efficiently as possible. Efficient framing can create additional spacing in wall cavities, reducing thermal breaks and insulation compaction. Also, environmentally preferable insulation is awarded in Materials & Resources (MR 2.2),

Low-flow showerheads, faucets and toilets contribute to energy savings as well as low water use appliances, such as clothes washers and dishwashers. Improving the lighting efficiency may also reduce cooling loads and the energy consumption associated with air–conditioning.

ENERGY & ATMOSPHERE

THE CREDITS

EA 1: Optimize Energy Performance	These credits require that the home be designed to meet the performance of the ENERGY STAR for Homes program. Higher levels of energy performance are recognized by modeling the energy performance of the home using the HERS modeling process.
EA 2: Insulation	These credits reward homes for improved thermal performance from insulation.
EA 3: Air Infiltration	These credits reward builders who use air-sealing techniques to tighten the envelope of new homes.
EA 4: Windows	These credits reward the selection and installation of windows with specifications that exceed the ENERGY STAR for Homes window requirements.
EA 5: Heating and Cooling Distribution System	These credits reward the installation of highly efficient distribution systems that are properly sized and have minimal air leaks.
EA 6: Space Heating and Cooling Equipment	These credits reward the installation of heating and cooling equipment that meets or exceeds the performance levels required by the ENERGY STAR for Homes national Builder Option Package.
EA 7: Water Heating	These credits reward the design and installation of efficient hot-water distribution systems and the selection of high-efficiency water heating equipment.
EA 8: Lighting	These credits reward the installation of ENERGY STAR–labeled light fixtures, compact fluorescent bulbs and exterior lighting-control equipment.
EA 9: Appliances	This credit rewards homes that install ENERGY STAR–labeled appliances.
EA 10: Renewable Energy	This credit rewards the installation of renewable-electricity generation systems that meet substantial portions of a home's annual electric load.
EA 11: Residential Refrigerant Management	These credits require the testing of the refrigerant charge and encourage the early selection of non-HCFC refrigerants in HVAC equipment.

ENERGY & ATMOSPHERE

The LEED for Homes Rating System allows two pathways to meet the requirements of energy performance:

Performance Pathway

- EA 1.1: ENERGY STAR for Homes—Meet the performance requirements of ENERGY STAR for Homes, including third-party inspections.
- EA 1.2: Exceptional Energy Performance.
- EA 7.1: Efficient Hot Water Distribution.
- EA 7.2: Pipe Insulation.
- EA 11.1: Refrigerant Charge Test.
- EA 11.2: Appropriate HVAC Refrigerants.

OR

Prescriptive Pathway

- EA 2–11

KEY TERMS

balancing damper	An adjustable plate that regulates airflow within ducts.
chlorofluorocarbon (CFC)	A chemical compound, once commonly used in refrigeration, that depletes the stratospheric ozone layer.
circulation loop	A system that returns cold water to the water heater (instead of down the drain) until hot water reaches the faucet. A circulation loop is one component of a structured plumbing system.
climate zone	In the U.S., one of eight regions as defined by the International Energy Conservation Code that characterize the temperature of an area of the country. Climate zone 1 is the hottest, and climate zone 8 is the coldest.
conditioned space	Interior area that utilizes any method of air-conditioning or heating to control temperature and/or humidity levels, usually measured in cubic feet.
ENERGY STAR home	A home built to a high standard of energy efficiency (at least 15% more efficient than the International Energy Conservation Code). For more information, visit www.energystar.gov/homes.

ENERGY STAR for Homes National Builder Option Package	A prescriptive-measures approach to achieving the ENERGY STAR for Homes certification.
envelope	See thermal envelope.
Home Energy Rating System (HERS) Index	A system for evaluating the energy efficiency of a home using an energy simulation model. A HERS index of 100 represents the energy efficiency of a home that meets basic IECC code requirements; each additional index point represents a 1% increase in energy use, and lower index numbers indicate the percentage savings in energy use.
hydrochlorofluorocarbon (HCFC)	A chemical compound used as a refrigerant. HCFCs deplete the stratospheric ozone layer, but to a lesser extent than chlorofluorocarbons (CFCs).
hydronic system	A heating or cooling system that uses circulating water as the heat-transfer medium, such as a boiler with hot water circulated through radiators.
infiltration degree-days	The sum of the heating degree-days and the cooling degree-days.
light fixture	Illumination that is permanently fixed to the home. A fluorescent light fixture has an integrated ballast. A compact fluorescent lamp (CFL) is not a light fixture.
RESCHECK	Developed by the U.S. Department of Energy, RESCHECK is an easy-to-use software program that determines whether a home's insulation levels meet the IECC (or appropriate local code) requirements. This free software can be downloaded from www.energycodes.gov/rescheck.
refrigerant	A fluid that absorbs heat from a reservoir at low temperatures and rejects heat at higher temperatures.
R-value	A measure of thermal resistance, defined as the number of watts lost per square meter at a given temperature difference. R-value is the inverse of U-value (that is, R = 1/U).

solar heat gain coefficient (SHGC)	A measure of how well a window blocks heat from the sun, expressed as a fraction of the heat from the sun that enters the window. A lower SHGC is generally preferable, particularly in hot climates.
solar window screen	Mesh used to block light and heat from the sun, as well as insects.
thermal bridge	A part of a building envelope that has high heat conductance, lowering the average R-value.
thermal envelope	The thermal enclosure created by the building exterior and insulation.
U-value	A measure of thermal conductivity (often used for windows) that is the inverse of R-value. A lower U-value means a more energy-efficient window. Also known as U-factor.

PRIMARY BENEFITS

- Reduces energy consumption.
- Reduces CO_2 production.
- Makes home more comfortable.
- Improves durability.

STANDARDS

Home Energy Rating System (HERS)

Residential Energy Services Network (RESNET)

International Energy Conservation Code (IECC), 2004 version

INTENT

Improve the overall energy performance of a home by meeting or exceeding the performance of an ENERGY STAR labeled home.

REQUIREMENTS

- Meet the performance requirements of the ENERGY STAR for Homes program, including third-party inspections. These can be met in two ways:
  - Build and certify the home according to the ENERGY STAR for Homes program;

  OR

  - Build the home to meet the performance levels of the ENERGY STAR for Homes program. The home does not need to be certified by the ENERGY STAR for Homes program. The home must also meet the following requirements:

    - Receive a qualified Home Energy Rating System (HERS) score;
    - Undergo a thermal bypass inspection;
    - Undergo a visual inspection of all installed energy efficiency measures; and
    - Pass performance tests for envelope tightness and duct tightness.

IMPLEMENTATION

- Meeting the national ENERGY STAR for Homes program requirements meets the requirements of this measure.

VERIFICATION & SUBMITTALS

PROJECT TEAM

- Present any equipment or product literature (for example, user manuals, brochures and specifications) related to the energy-consuming systems and energy-saving components (such as HVAC equipment, windows, insulation and appliances) to the Green Rater.

- Include all equipment literature in the occupant's operations and maintenance manual.

GREEN RATER

- Complete the verification requirements for an ENERGY STAR home, including thermal bypass (insulation) inspection, envelope air leakage testing with a blower door, and duct leakage testing with a duct pressurization fan.

- Visually verify all energy-consuming systems and energy-saving components at the homesite. Document the relevant metrics (for example, efficiencies, R-values and percentage of fluorescent lights) and provide them to the energy rater for modeling.

- Conduct the necessary modeling to produce a HERS Index Score, or have an independent energy rater conduct the necessary modeling. Verify that the HERS Index Score for the home meets or exceeds the prerequisite.

- Include a copy of the HERS rating report in the project documentation file and the occupant's operations and maintenance manual.

DOCUMENTATION & CALCULATIONS

- None beyond those performed by the HERS energy modeling software.

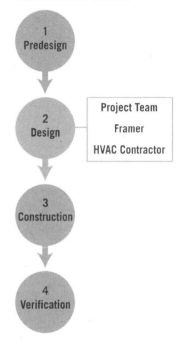

TIMELINE/TEAM

1 Predesign

2 Design — Project Team / Framer / HVAC Contractor

3 Construction

4 Verification

NOTES

- LEED for Homes addresses overall energy performance with two interrelated measures, EA 1.1 and EA 1.2. A home that has exceptional energy performance under EA 1.2 will automatically demonstrate compliance with the prerequisite, EA 1.1.

- A project receiving points for this credit must skip credits EA 2–6, 7.3 and 8–10.

PRIMARY BENEFITS

- Reduces energy consumption.
- Reduces CO_2 production.
- Makes home more comfortable.
- Improves durability.

STANDARDS

Home Energy Rating System (HERS)

Residential Energy Services Network (RESNET)

International Energy Conservation Code (IECC), 2004 version

INTENT

Improve the overall energy performance of a home by meeting or exceeding the performance of an ENERGY STAR labeled home.

REQUIREMENTS

- Exceed the performance levels of ENERGY STAR for Homes using the HERS Index.

- Up to 34 points can be achieved by exceeding the thresholds for ENERGY STAR for Homes. Projects pursing this pathway will need to receive a HERS Index Score. The HERS Index Score will be applied to a calculation that is based on two groupings of the IECC Climate Zones (1–5 for Southern and 6–8 for Northern). In climate zones 1–5, a project will start to earn points when it achieves a HERS Index Score of 84 or better. In climate zones 6–8, a project will start to earn points when it achieves a HERS Index Score of 79 or better.

IMPLEMENTATION

- Build the home with energy efficiency measures that exceed the minimum performance levels required for the national ENERGY STAR for Homes program.

- Use the LEED for Homes Checklist, which automatically calculates the number of LEED points achieved with an input of the HERS Index Score and the appropriate climate zone for the project.

VERIFICATION & SUBMITTALS

GREEN RATER

- Conduct the necessary modeling to produce a HERS Index Score, or have an independent energy rater conduct the necessary modeling. Verify that the HERS Index Score for the home exceeds the prerequisite.

- Include a copy of the HERS rating report in the project documentation file and the occupant's operations and maintenance manual.

DOCUMENTATION & CALCULATIONS

Southern (IECC Climate Zones 1–5)

LEED Points = { [Log (100 - HERS Index)] / 0.024 } - 48.3

Northern (IECC Climate Zones 6–8)

LEED Points = { [Log (100 - HERS Index)] / 0.021 } - 60.8

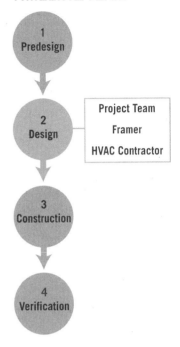

TIMELINE/TEAM

1 Predesign

2 Design

Project Team
Framer
HVAC Contractor

3 Construction

4 Verification

NOTES

- LEED for Homes addresses overall energy performance with two interrelated measures, EA 1.1 and EA 1.2. A home that has exceptional energy performance under EA 1.2 will automatically demonstrate compliance with the prerequisite, EA 1.1.

- The closer a home moves toward net zero energy consumption, the higher the number of LEED for Homes points that will be awarded to the project.

PRIMARY BENEFITS

- Reduces energy use for heating and cooling the home.

STANDARDS

None

INTENT

Design and install insulation to minimize heat transfer and thermal bridging.

REQUIREMENTS

- Meet all of the following:

  ○ Install insulation that meets or exceeds the insulation performance values requirements listed in Chapter 4 of the 2004 International Energy Conservation Code.

  ○ Install insulation to meet Grade II specifications set by the National Home Energy Rating Standards. Installation must be verified by an energy rater or Green Rater conducting a predrywall thermal bypass inspection.

  ○ If using structural insulated panels (SIPs) or insulated concrete forms (ICFs), either for the whole home or part of the home, the installer must perform a thermal inspection using the ENERGY STAR Structural Insulated Panel Visual Inspection Form.

IMPLEMENTATION

- Installing installation so it touches all six surfaces of the cavity ensures the performance of the insulation.

- Several insulation products are available today. The goal is to choose the type of insulation that provides the best value for the performance desired.

VERIFICATION & SUBMITTALS

PROJECT TEAM

- If using RESCHECK to demonstrate overall performance, provide calculations to the Green Rater.

GREEN RATER

- Visually inspect the installation of insulation, per the thermal bypass inspection checklist (see EA 2 Figure 1. ENERGY STAR Thermal Bypass Inspection Checklist in the LEED Reference Guide for Homes, 2008), to confirm that the requirements have been met.

- If manual calculations or the RESCHECK software is used to demonstrate overall performance, visually verify the calculations.

DOCUMENTATION & CALCULATIONS

- None is needed unless the insulation values are averaged. In that case, an overall thermal conductance can be calculated by hand or demonstrated using RESCHECK software.

TIMELINE/TEAM

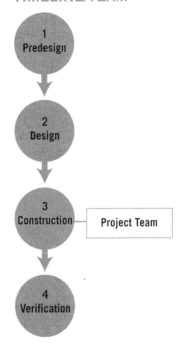

1 Predesign

2 Design

3 Construction — Project Team

4 Verification

NOTES

- A project receiving points for EA 1 would not use this pathway, and vice versa. A project pursuing this measure must follow the prescriptive pathway and all of the associated prerequisites in EA 2–10. Prerequisite EA 1.1 should be skipped.

PRIMARY BENEFITS

- Improves thermal performance of the home.

INTENT

Design and install insulation to minimize heat transfer and thermal bridging.

STANDARDS

National Home Energy Rating

2004 International Energy Conservation Code

REQUIREMENTS

- Meet all of the following:
  - Install insulation that exceeds the insulation performance values requirements listed in Chapter 4 of the 2004 International Energy Conservation Code by at least 5%.
  - Install insulation to meet Grade I specifications set by the National Home Energy Rating Standards. Installation must be verified by an energy rater or Green Rater conducting a predrywall thermal bypass inspection.
  - If using structural insulated panels (SIPs) or insulated concrete forms (ICFs), either for the whole home or part of the home, the installer must perform a thermal inspection using the ENERGY STAR Structural Insulated Panel Visual Inspection Form.

IMPLEMENTATION

- Ensure that the insulation completely fills the cavity, with a minimum of voids, and that the insulation touches all six sides of the cavity.

VERIFICATION & SUBMITTALS

PROJECT TEAM
- If using RESCHECK to demonstrate overall performance, provide calculations to the Green Rater.

GREEN RATER
- Visually inspect the installation of the insulation, per the thermal bypass inspection checklist (see the LEED for Homes Reference Guide, 2008, page 181), to confirm that the requirements have been met.

- If manual calculations or RESCHECK software is used to demonstrate overall performance, visually verify the calculations.

DOCUMENTATION & CALCULATIONS

- None is needed unless the insulation values are averaged. In that case, an overall thermal conductance can be calculated by hand or demonstrated using RESCHECK software.

- If not all of the insulation exceeds the requirements by 5%, the requirements can still be met by demonstrating that the overall thermal conductance value (UAo) exceeds code by 5% using RESCHECK software.

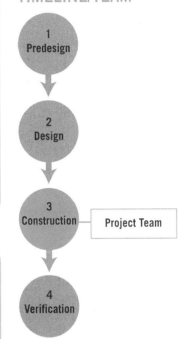

TIMELINE/TEAM

1 Predesign

2 Design

3 Construction — Project Team

4 Verification

NOTES

- Quality installation (with minimal voids, meaning the insulation touches all six surfaces) can improve the performance of the insulation.

- A project receiving points for EA 1 is not eligible for this credit, and vice versa. A project pursuing this credit must follow the prescriptive pathway and all of the associated prerequisites in EA 2–10. Prerequisite EA 1.1 should be skipped.

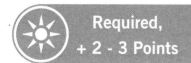
EA 3: Air Infiltration

PRIMARY BENEFITS

- The energy performance of the home is improved.

- More even temperatures throughout the home result in higher homeowner comfort.

STANDARDS

None

GOOD, BETTER, BEST

EA Prerequisite 3.1: Reduced Envelope Leakage (Required)
EA Credit 3.2: Greatly Reduced Envelope Leakage (2 points)
EA Credit 3.3: Minimal Envelope Leakage (3 points)

INTENT

Design and install insulation to minimize heat transfer and thermal bridging.

REQUIREMENTS

- Meet the air leakage requirements of the IECC Climate Zone where the home is being built (see chart below).

- Have an envelope-tightness performance test (blower door test) performed by an energy rater.

- The results of the envelope-tightness performance test will be evaluated and points will be awarded from the chart below.

Table 1 from the LEED for Homes Reference Guide, 2008. Page 185. Air Leakage Requirements.

	Performance Requirements (in ACH 50)			
LEED Criteria	**IECC Climate Zones 1–2**	**IECC Climate Zones 3–4**	**IECC Climate Zones 5–7**	**IECC Climate Zone 8**
EA 3.1, (Required)	7.0	6.0	5.0	4.0
EA 3.2, (2 points)	5.0	4.3	3.5	2.8
EA 3.3, (3 points)	3.0	2.5	2.0	1.5

IMPLEMENTATION

- The builder will need to incorporate a strategy to create a tight envelope. Generally, sealing all penetrations through the shell of the home will reduce leakage. This needs to be done during construction, because it is very difficult to find and seal leaks after drywall has been installed.

VERIFICATION & SUBMITTALS

GREEN RATER

● Perform a blower door depressurization test on the home to determine the envelope leakage.

DOCUMENTATION & CALCULATIONS

● None is needed if the blower door test produces a result in ACH 50. The ACH 50 value can be calculated using the following formula:

○ ACH 50 = CFM 50 X 60 Minutes/Hour + Volume, Where the Volume Is Measured in Cubic Feet.

TIMELINE/TEAM

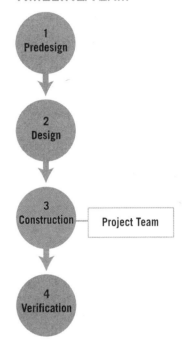

NOTES

● It is just as important not to underventilate a home, for health reasons, as it is not to overventilate a home, for energy performance reasons.

● A project receiving points for EA 1 is not eligible for credit EA 3.2 and EA 3.3, and vice versa. A project pursuing these credits must follow the prescriptive pathway and all of the associated prerequisites in EA 2–10. Prerequisite EA 1.1 should be skipped.

PRIMARY BENEFITS

- Improving the window performance may also reduce heating and/or cooling loads and the energy associated with operating heating and cooling equipment.

STANDARDS

National Fenestration Rating Council (NFRC) ratings

GOOD, BETTER, BEST

EA Prerequisite 4.1: Good Windows (Required)
EA Credit 4.2: Enhanced Windows (2 points)
EA Credit 4.3: Exceptional Windows (3 points)

INTENT

Maximize the energy performance of windows.

REQUIREMENTS

- Meet all of the following requirements:
  - Select and install windows and glass doors that have an NFRC rating that meets or exceeds the requirements of the ENERGY STAR for Homes national Builder Option Package (see the table below).
  - The ratio of skylight glazing to conditioned floor area may not exceed 3%.

- An example: A 2,500-square-foot home would be able to have 75 square feet of skylights. The skylights must meet ENERGY STAR performance requirements but are exempt from the requirements in the table.
  - Homes in the Northern or North/Central climate zones that exceed the threshold of 18% window-to-floor area ratio (WFA) must meet a more rigorous U-factor requirement.

- The formula is U-factor = [0.18 / WFA] X [U-factor from the table].
  - Homes in the Southern or South/Central climate zones that exceed the threshold of 18% WFA must meet more rigorous solar heat gain coefficient (SHGC) requirements.

- The formula is SHGC = [0.18 / WFA] X [SHGC from the table].
  - Up to 0.75% of the window-to-floor area may be used for decorative glass or skylight area that does not need to meet the U-factor or SHGC requirements.

Table 1 from the LEED for Homes Reference Guide, 2008. Page 190. ENERGY STAR Requirements for Windows and Glass Doors.

LEED Criteria	Metric	Northern	North Central	South Central	Southern
EA 4.1: Good Windows, (Required)	U-factor SHGC	≤ 0.35 Any	≤ 0.40 ≤ 0.45	≤ 0.40 ≤ 0.40	≤0.55 ≤ 0.35
EA 4.2: Enhanced Windows, (2 points)	U-factor SHGC	≤ 0.31 Any	≤ 0.35 ≤ 0.40	≤ 0.35 ≤ 0.35	≤ 0.55 ≤ 0.33
EA 4.3: Exceptional Windows, (3 points)	U-factor SHGC	≤ 0.28 Any	≤ 0.32 ≤ 0.40	≤ 0.32 ≤ 0.30	≤ 0.55 ≤ 0.30

Exemplary Performance: Not eligible, but homes that use windows that exceed the performance specifications in EA 4.3 may want to use the Performance Pathway, because that pathway will reflect the windows' higher performance.

IMPLEMENTATION

- The best window still does not perform as well as an average insulated wall. Therefore, reducing the number of windows can improve the thermal performance of a home more than improving the performance of a window can.

- Choose windows with good thermal and solar heat gain performance.

VERIFICATION & SUBMITTALS

PROJECT TEAM

- Present any equipment literature (for example, brochures and specifications) to the Green Rater.

- Present any calculations related to excess window area, solar screens, or U-value and SHGC averaging to the Green Rater.

GREEN RATER

- Visually verify (using brochures, specifications, window labels and so on) that the window specifications meet the requirements.

- Visually verify any calculations related to the windows.

DOCUMENTATION & CALCULATIONS

- WFA calculation:
  - WFA = Total Glazing Area / Total Conditioned Floor Area

- Formula for Northern and North/Central is U-factor = [0.18 / WFA] X [U-factor from the table]

- Formula for Southern and South/Central is SHGC = [0.18 / WFA] X [SHGC from the table]

- Example for window performance in Northern and North/Central:
  - The home has a WFA of 22% and needs to pass prerequisite performance.
  - The windows must have a U-factor of 0.29 (0.29 = [0.18 / 0.22] X 0.35).

- Example for window performance in Southern and South/Central:
  - The home has a WFA of 25% and needs to pass prerequisite performance.
  - The windows must have a SHGC of 0.25 (0.25 = [0.18 / 0.25] X 0.35).

- Up to 0.75% of the window-to-floor area may be used for decorative glass or skylight area that does not meet the U-factor or SHGC requirements.

TIMELINE/TEAM

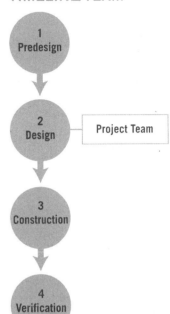

NOTES

- Window performance is critical to achieving a superior energy-efficient home. Windows with smaller U-factor numbers are higher-performing windows; therefore, the lower the U-factor number the better the window's performance.

- The SHGC is a measure of how well a window blocks heat from the sun, expressed as a fraction of the heat from the sun that enters the window. A low SHGC is generally preferable, particularly in hot climates.

- A project receiving points for EA 1 is not eligible for credit EA 4.2 and EA 4.3, and vice versa. A project pursuing these credits must follow the prescriptive pathway and all of the associated prerequisites in EA 2–10. Prerequisite EA 1.1 should be skipped.

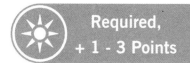

PRIMARY BENEFITS

- Improves energy performance of the heating and cooling distribution system.

- Improved homeowner comfort.

STANDARDS

None

GOOD, BETTER, BEST

EA Prerequisite 5.1: Reduced Distribution Losses (Required)
EA Credit 5.2: Greatly Reduced Distribution Losses (2 points)
AND/OR
EA Credit 5.3: Minimal Distribution Losses (1 point for Nonducted HVAC Systems or 3 points for Forced-Air Systems)

INTENT

Minimize energy consumption due to thermal bridges and/or leaks in the heating and cooling distribution system.

REQUIREMENTS

There are two pathways to achieve this measure: Forced-Air Systems and Nonducted HVAC Systems.

Forced-Air Systems:
- Meet the following for EA 5.1 (prerequisite):
  - Limit the duct leakage rate to outside the conditioned envelope to ≤ 4.0 cfm at 25 Pascals per 100 square feet of conditioned floor area. Duct testing needs to be performed unless the home meets EA 5.3 (b) or (c).
  - Ducts cannot be installed in exterior walls unless extra insulation is installed to maintain the overall UA for an exterior wall without ducts. Wall cavities may not be used as ducts.
- Meet the following for EA 5.2 (2 points):
  - Limit the duct leakage rate to outside the conditioned envelope to ≤ 3.0 cfm at 25 Pascals per 100 square feet of conditioned floor area.
  OR
- Meet one of the following for EA 5.3 (3 points):
  - Limit the duct leakage rate to outside the conditioned envelope to ≤1.0 cfm at 25 Pascals per 100 square feet of conditioned floor area.
  - Locate the air-handler unit and all ductwork within the conditioned envelope and minimize envelope leakage (that is, meet the requirements of EA 3.3).
  - Locate the air-handler unit and all ductwork visibly within the conditioned spaces (there should be no ductwork hidden in walls, chases, floors or ceilings).

Nonducted HVAC Systems (Hydronic Systems):
- Meet the following for EA 5.1 (prerequisite):
  - Use at least R-3 insulation around distribution pipes in unconditioned spaces.
- Meet the following for EA 5.2 (2 points):
  - Keep the system, including all equipment and distribution pipes, within the conditioned envelope.
- Meet the following for EA 5.3 (1 point):
  - Incorporate an outdoor reset control that modulates distribution water temperature based on outdoor air temperature.

IMPLEMENTATION

- Seal and insulate ducts and insulate nonducted distribution systems.

VERIFICATION & SUBMITTALS

PROJECT TEAM

- Include all equipment literature in the occupant's operations and maintenance manual.

GREEN RATER

For EA 5.1:

- Forced-Air Systems:
  - Perform duct leakage testing that meets the requirements.
  - Visually verify that the duct installation and insulation meet the requirements.

- Nonducted HVAC Systems:
  - Visually verify that the requirements are met.

For EA 5.2 and EA 5.3:

- Forced-Air Systems:
  - Perform duct leakage testing that meets the requirements.
  - Visually verify that the duct installation and insulation meet the requirements.

- Nonducted HVAC Systems:
  - Visually verify that the requirements are met.

DOCUMENTATION & CALCULATIONS

None

TIMELINE/TEAM

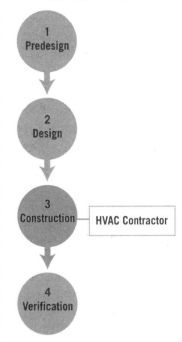

NOTES

- A project receiving points for EA 1 is not eligible for credit EA 5.2 and EA 5.3, and vice versa. A project pursuing these credits must follow the prescriptive pathway and all of the associated prerequisites in EA 2–10. Prerequisite EA 1.1 should be skipped.

- When the HVAC and heating and cooling system is being designed (EA 5, 6: EQ 4, 6) EQ 10.1 must be taken into consideration.

PRIMARY BENEFITS

- Higher-efficiency equipment reduces the cost to provide heating and cooling in the home.

STANDARDS

None

GOOD, BETTER, BEST

EA Prerequisite 6.1: Good HVAC Design and Installation (required)
EA Credit 6.2: High-Efficiency HVAC (2 points)
EA Credit 6.3: Very High-Efficiency HVAC (maximum of 4 points)

INTENT

Reduce energy consumption associated with the heating and cooling system.

REQUIREMENTS

To earn the full points for this measure, both the heating and cooling systems must meet the requirement. If only one of the systems qualifies, only half the points can be earned.

Homes that are built without a heating or cooling system must use the EA Performance Pathway. They must be modeled under EA 1 using the default efficiency allowed in both the reference and rated homes. The modeling will reflect the energy performance from home orientation that the Prescriptive Pathway does not recognize.

- Meet all of the following requirements for EA 6.1 (prerequisite):
  - Use ACCA Manual J or an equivalent computation method to determine the heating and cooling loads.
  - Use ACCA Manual S to size the heating and cooling equipment based on the Manual J calculation.
  - Select, design and install the HVAC equipment that meets the performance specifications in the credit (see the LEED for Homes Reference Guide, 2008, page 202, for specifications).
  - Install an ENERGY STAR programmable thermostat (Heat pumps and hydronic systems are exempt).
  - Homes with heat pumps and programmable thermostats must have adaptive recovery.

- Meet the following requirements for EA 6.2 (2 points):
  - Install efficient heating and cooling equipment that exceeds the minimum prescriptive performance levels (see the LEED for Homes Reference Guide, 2008, page 202, for points).
  OR

- Meet the following requirements for EA 6.3 (maximum of 4 points):
  - Install efficient heating and cooling equipment that exceeds the minimum prescriptive performance levels (see the LEED for Homes Reference Guide, 2008, page 202, for points).
  - Any piping designed as part of the heat pump system to carry water that is well above (or below) the thermostatic temperature settings in the home must have R-4 insulation around the piping.
  - The maximum of four points is available for heat pump systems only. Furnace and boiler systems can earn only a maximum of three points.

EA 6: Space Heating and Cooling Equipment

IMPLEMENTATION

● Placing the space heating and cooling equipment in conditioned spaces can improve the performance of the equipment.

● The choice of air filter should be made prior to duct design, to ensure adequate air flow.

VERIFICATION & SUBMITTALS

TRADE

● Provide design calculations related to the HVAC design to the builder or project team leader.

● Provide any HVAC system equipment literature (such as user manuals, brochures and specifications) to the builder or project team leader.

● Sign an Accountability Form to indicate that the system was designed and installed according to the prerequisite.

PROJECT TEAM

● Present design calculations related to the HVAC design to the Green Rater.

● Present any HVAC system equipment literature (such as user manuals, brochures and specifications) to the Green Rater.

● Include HVAC equipment literature in the occupant's operations and maintenance manual.

GREEN RATER

● Visually verify that all HVAC design calculations are completed.

● Visually verify (using equipment literature, labels and so on) the type of equipment installed and its efficiency.

● Verify that an Accountability Form has been signed by the responsible party.

DOCUMENTATION & CALCULATIONS

● Other than ACCA Manual J, no other calculations are necessary.

TIMELINE/TEAM

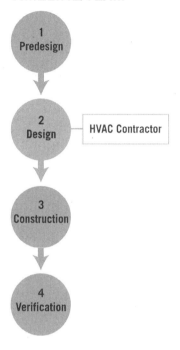

1 Predesign

2 Design — HVAC Contractor

3 Construction

4 Verification

NOTES

● A project receiving points for EA 1 is not eligible for credit EA 6.2 and EA 6.3, and vice versa. A project pursuing these credits must follow the prescriptive pathway and all of the associated prerequisites in EA 2–10. Prerequisite EA 1.1 should be skipped.

● When the HVAC and heating and cooling system is being designed (EA 5, 6: EQ 4, 6) EQ 10.1 must be taken into consideration.

PRIMARY BENEFITS

- Reduces water use.

- Reduces energy use.

- Speeds delivery of hot water to fixtures.

STANDARDS

None

INTENT

Reduce energy consumption associated with the domestic hot-water system, including improving the efficiency of both the hot-water system design and the layout of the fixtures in the home.

REQUIREMENTS

- Design and install an energy-efficient hot-water distribution system. Select one of the following:
  - Structured plumbing system (1 point):
    - Demand-controlled circulation loop.
    - Insulated to R-4.
    - Branch lines cannot exceed 10 feet in length and cannot exceed 1/2-inch nominal diameter.
    - A push button must be used in each full bathroom and the kitchen, and the system must have an automatic pump shutoff.

    OR
  - Structured plumbing system (2 points):
    - Demand-controlled circulation loop.
    - Insulated to R-4.
    - Total length of the loop is less than 40 linear feet for one-story homes. Add two times the ceiling height for two-story homes and four times for three- or four-story homes.
    - Branch lines cannot exceed 10 feet in length and cannot exceed 1/2-inch nominal diameter.
    - A push button must be used in each full bathroom and the kitchen, and the system must have an automatic pump shutoff.

    OR
  - Central manifold system (2 points):
    - The central manifold panel can be no more than 6 feet from the water heater.
    - The trunk line must be insulated to R-4.
    - No branch line from the central manifold to any fixture may exceed 20 feet in one-story homes. Add one times the ceiling height for two-story homes and add two times the ceiling height for three- and four-story homes.
    - Branch lines must be a maximum of one-half inch in nominal diameter.

    OR
  - Compact design of conventional system (2 points):
    - No branch line from the water heater to any fixture may exceed 20 feet in one-story homes. Add one time the ceiling height for two-story homes and add two times the ceiling height for three- and four-story homes.
    - Branch lines must be a maximum of one-half inch in nominal diameter.

IMPLEMENTATION

- Design a home with short runs by locating the water heating system centrally.

VERIFICATION & SUBMITTALS

TRADE

- Sign an Accountability Form to indicate that the hot-water distribution system is installed according to the credit requirements.

PROJECT TEAM

- Include all equipment literature in the occupant's operations and maintenance manual.

GREEN RATER

- Visually verify the design of the hot-water distribution system.

- Verify that an Accountability Form has been signed by the responsible party.

DOCUMENTATION & CALCULATIONS

- Calculate the length from the water heater to the farthest fixtures in actual linear feet of piping.

TIMELINE/TEAM

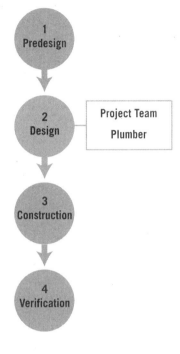

NOTES

- EA 7.1 and 7.2 are available to every project, whether the performance approach (EA 1) or the prescriptive approach (EA 2–10) is used.

PRIMARY BENEFITS

- Reduces energy loss in hot-water lines.

STANDARDS

None

INTENT

Reduce energy consumption associated with the domestic hot-water system, including improving the efficiency of both the hot-water system design and the layout of the fixtures in the home.

REQUIREMENTS

- Insulate all domestic hot-water lines with R-4 insulation.

IMPLEMENTATION

- Insulating the hot-water lines needs to take place before the wall cavity is covered with drywall.

VERIFICATION & SUBMITTALS

GREEN RATER

- Visually verify that pipes are insulated according to the credit requirements.

DOCUMENTATION & CALCULATIONS

- Measure pipe length.

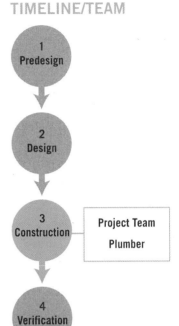

1 Predesign

2 Design

3 Construction — Project Team Plumber

4 Verification

NOTES

- EA 7.1 and 7.2 are available to every project, whether the performance approach (EA 1) or the prescriptive approach (EA 2–10) is used.

PRIMARY BENEFITS

- Reduces energy use.

STANDARDS

None

INTENT

Reduce energy consumption associated with the domestic hot-water system, including improving the efficiency of both the hot-water system design and the layout of the fixtures in the home.

REQUIREMENTS

- Design and install energy-efficient water heating equipment. Select one measure from Table 1 on page 209 of the LEED for Homes Reference Guide, 2008.

Table 1 from the LEED for Homes Reference Guide, 2008. Page 209. High-Efficiency Water Heating Equipment.

Water heater type and efficiency requirement	Description	Points
Gas water heaters		
EF ≥ 0.53 (80 gallon)	High-efficiency storage water heater	1
EF ≥ 0.57 (60 gallon)	High-efficiency storage water heater	1
EF ≥ 0.61 (40 gallon)	High-efficiency storage water heater	1
EF ≥ 0.8	Storage or tankless water heater	2
CAE ≥ 0.8	Combination water and space heaters	2
Electric water heaters		
EF ≥ 0.89 (80 gallon)	High-efficiency storage water heater	1
EF ≥ 0.92 (50 gallon)	High-efficiency storage water heater	1
EF ≥ 0.93 (40 gallon)	High-efficiency storage water heater	1
EF ≥ 0.99EF ≥ 2.0	Tankless water heater	2
	Heat pump water heater	3
Solar water heaters (backup)		
≥ 40% of annual DHW load	With preheat tank	2
≥ 60% of annual DHW load	With preheat tank	3
EF = Energy factor. Energy factors for equipment from various manufacturers are available at http://www.gamanet.org/gama/inforesources.nsf/vContentEntries/Product+Directories.		
CAE = Combined annual efficiency.		

IMPLEMENTATION

- New water heating products are being introduced continually. Researching the latest available products can result in high performance while keeping costs at a minimum. Install the most efficient system the project team or homeowner can afford.

VERIFICATION & SUBMITTALS

TRADE

- Provide any equipment literature related to the hot-water distribution system (such as user manuals, brochures and specifications) to the builder or project team leader.

- For a solar hot-water heater, provide calculations to the builder or project team leader demonstrating the percentage of the annual domestic hot-water load being met.

PROJECT TEAM

- Present any equipment literature related to the hot-water distribution system (such as user manuals, brochures and specifications) to the Green Rater.

- Include equipment literature in the occupant's operations and maintenance manual.

- For a solar hot-water heater, present calculations to the Green Rater demonstrating the percentage of the annual domestic hot-water load being met.

GREEN RATER

- Visually verify (using equipment literature, labels and so on) the type of equipment installed and its efficiency.

- For a solar hot-water heater, visually verify that the calculations meet the requirements.

DOCUMENTATION & CALCULATIONS

None

TIMELINE/TEAM

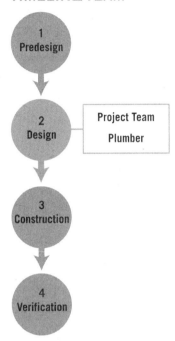

NOTES

- A project receiving points for EA 1 is not eligible for EA 7.3, and vice versa. A project pursuing EA 7.3 must follow the prescriptive pathway and meet all of the prerequisites in EA 2–10. Prerequisite EA 1.1 should be skipped.

PRIMARY BENEFITS

- Lighting can use significant amounts of energy. Incorporating strategies that use ENERGY STAR–labeled fluorescent lighting will reduce energy consumption.

STANDARDS

None

INTENT

Reduce energy consumption with interior and exterior lighting.

REQUIREMENTS

- Install at least four ENERGY STAR–labeled light fixtures or ENERGY STAR–labeled compact fluorescent lightbulbs (CFLs) in high-use rooms.

IMPLEMENTATION

- Select high-use areas to install the fixtures or lightbulbs, such as the kitchen, dining room, living room, family room and hallways.

EA 8: Lighting
EA Prerequisite 8.1: ENERGY STAR Lights

Exemplary Performance No

VERIFICATION & SUBMITTALS

PROJECT TEAM

● Include all equipment literature in the occupant's operations and maintenance manual.

GREEN RATER

● Visually verify the ENERGY STAR lights in the home.

DOCUMENTATION & CALCULATIONS

None

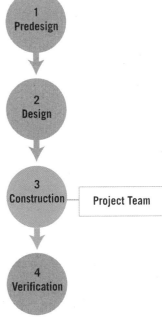

NOTES

● A project receiving points for EA 1 is not eligible for this credit, and vice versa. A project pursuing this credit must follow the prescriptive pathway and meet all the associated prerequisites in EA 2–10. Prerequisite EA 1.1 should be skipped.

PRIMARY BENEFITS

- Lighting can use significant amounts of energy. Incorporating strategies that use ENERGY STAR–labeled fluorescent lighting will reduce energy consumption.

STANDARDS

None

INTENT

Reduce energy consumption with interior and exterior lighting.

REQUIREMENTS

- Choose either EA 8.2 or EA 8.3.

- Select and install one or more of the following:

  o Interior lighting (0.5 point):
    - Install an additional three ENERGY STAR–labeled light fixtures or ENERGY STAR–labeled compact fluorescent lightbulbs (CFLs) in high-use rooms.

  o Exterior lighting (1 point):
    - All exterior lighting must have motion-sensor controls; and/or
    - All exterior lighting must have integrated photovoltaic cells (solar cell lights).

    - The following lights are exempt:
      o Emergency lighting;
      o Lighting required by code for health and safety purposes; and
      o Lighting used for eye adaption near covered vehicle entrances or exits.

IMPLEMENTATION

- Select high-use areas to install the fixtures or lightbulbs, such as the kitchen, dining room, living room, family room and hallways.

VERIFICATION & SUBMITTALS

PROJECT TEAM

- Include all equipment literature in the occupant's operations and maintenance manual.

GREEN RATER

- For interior lighting, visually verify ENERGY STAR lights.

- For exterior lighting, visually verify motion sensors and photovoltaic lights.

DOCUMENTATION & CALCULATIONS

None

TIMELINE/TEAM

1 Predesign

2 Design

3 Construction — Project Team

4 Verification

NOTES

- A project receiving points for EA 1 is not eligible for this credit, and vice versa. A project pursuing this credit must follow the prescriptive pathway and meet all the associated prerequisites in EA 2–10. Prerequisite EA 1.1 should be skipped.

PRIMARY BENEFITS

- Lighting can use significant amounts of energy. Incorporating strategies that use ENERGY STAR–labeled fluorescent lighting will reduce energy consumption.

STANDARDS

None

INTENT

Reduce energy consumption with interior and exterior lighting.

REQUIREMENTS

- Choose either EA 8.2 or EA 8.3.

- Install an ENERGY STAR Advanced Lighting Package using only ENERGY STAR–labeled fixtures. The Advanced Lighting Package consists of a minimum of 60% ENERGY STAR–qualified hard-wired fixtures and 100% ENERGY STAR–qualified fans, if any are installed.

  OR

- Install ENERGY STAR–labeled lamps such that 80% of all lamps in the home are ENERGY STAR–labeled. All ceiling fans must be ENERGY STAR–labeled.

Exemplary Performance: Projects can earn one ID point for the use of 90% ENERGY STAR–labeled lighting fixtures and 100% ENERGY STAR–labeled ceiling fans.

IMPLEMENTATION

- Select high-use areas to install the fixtures or lightbulbs, such as the kitchen, dining room, living room, family room and hallways.

VERIFICATION & SUBMITTALS

PROJECT TEAM

- Include all equipment literature in the occupant's operations and maintenance manual.

- Present calculations to the Green Rater demonstrating the percentage of light fixtures or lamps that are ENERGY STAR–labeled.

GREEN RATER

- Visually verify the ENERGY STAR lights in the home.

- Visually verify the calculations for the percentage of ENERGY STAR–labeled lights in the home.

DOCUMENTATION & CALCULATIONS

- Calculate the percentage of the home's light fixtures that are ENERGY STAR–labeled.

TIMELINE/TEAM

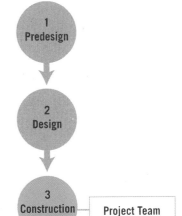

NOTES

- A project receiving points for EA 1 is not eligible for this credit, and vice versa. A project pursuing this credit must follow the prescriptive pathway and meet all the associated prerequisites in EA 2–10. Prerequisite EA 1.1 should be skipped.

PRIMARY BENEFITS

- Reduces energy consumption.

- Reduces water usage for clothes washers.

STANDARDS

None

EA Credit 9.1: High-Efficiency Appliances (maximum of 2 points)
EA Credit 9.2: Water-Efficient Clothes Washer (1 point)

INTENT

Reduce appliance energy consumption.

REQUIREMENTS

EA 9.1, High-Efficiency Appliances:

- Install appliances from the list below. To receive points for one type of appliance, every appliance of that type in the home must qualify.

  - ENERGY STAR–labeled refrigerator(s) (1 point);
  - ENERGY STAR–labeled ceiling fans (minimum of one in the living or family room and one per bedroom) (0.5 point);
  - ENERGY STAR–labeled dishwasher(s) that use 6.0 gallons or less per cycle (0.5 point); and
  - ENERGY STAR–labeled clothes washer(s) (0.5 point).

EA 9.2, Water-Efficient Clothes Washer:

- Install a clothes washer with a modified energy factor (MEF) of ≥ 2.0 and a water factor (WF) of < 5.5. A clothes washer that meets these requirements will earn this point in addition to the 0.5 point in EA 9.1.

Exemplary Performance: Projects that have followed the Performance Pathway of EA 1.2 can earn ID points for meeting EA 9.1 (d), for 0.5 point, and EA 9.2, for 1 point.

IMPLEMENTATION

- Select the most energy- and water-efficient appliances within the project budget.

VERIFICATION & SUBMITTALS

PROJECT TEAM

- Present any equipment literature related to the appliances (such as user manuals, brochures and specifications) to the Green Rater.

- Include all appliance literature in the occupant's operations and maintenance manual.

GREEN RATER

- Visually verify (using equipment literature, labels and such) the type of equipment installed and its efficiency.

DOCUMENTATION & CALCULATIONS

None

TIMELINE/TEAM

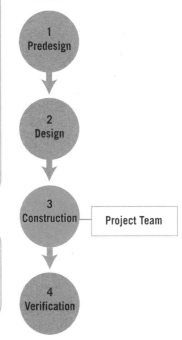

NOTES

- A project receiving points for EA 1 is not eligible for this credit, and vice versa. A project pursuing this credit must follow the prescriptive pathway and meet all the associated prerequisites in EA 2–10. Prerequisite EA 1.1 should be skipped.

- Projects that have followed the Performance Pathway of EA 1.2 can earn ID points for meeting EA 9.1 (d), for 0.5 point, and EA 9.2, for 1 additional point.

PRIMARY BENEFITS

- Generating electrical energy on-site reduces dependency on electrical power from nonrenewable sources.

- Renewable energy systems reduce CO_2 generation.

STANDARDS

The 2006 Mortgage Industry National Home Energy Rating Standards (HERS) Guidelines

INTENT

Reduce consumption of nonrenewable energy sources by encouraging the installation and operation of renewable electric generation systems.

REQUIREMENTS

- Design and install a renewable electricity generating system.

- Use energy modeling to estimate both the energy supplied by the system and the annual reference electrical load.

  - Annual reference electrical load is defined as the amount of electricity that a typical home would use in a typical year. It is to be determined using the procedures in the 2006 Mortgage Industry National Home Energy Rating Standards Guidelines.

IMPLEMENTATION

- Due to the cost of implementing a renewable energy system, the project team should address all other energy efficiency options first. A home that is not energy efficient is not made better by incorporating a renewable energy system.

VERIFICATION & SUBMITTALS

TRADE

- Provide any equipment literature related to the renewable energy system (such as user manuals, brochures and specifications) to the builder or project team leader.
- Provide calculations and/or modeling results to the builder or project team leader demonstrating the percentage of annual reference electrical load being met.
- Sign an Accountability Form indicating that the renewable energy system installed corresponds to the calculations provided.

PROJECT TEAM

- Present any equipment literature related to the renewable energy system (such as user manuals, brochures and specifications) to the Green Rater.
- Present calculations and/or modeling results to the Green Rater demonstrating the percentage of annual reference electrical load being met by the renewable energy system.
- Include equipment literature in the occupant's operations and maintenance manual.

GREEN RATER

- Visually verify the renewable energy system on-site.
- Visually verify that the calculations meet the requirements.
- Verify that an Accountability Form has been signed by the responsible party.

TIMELINE/TEAM

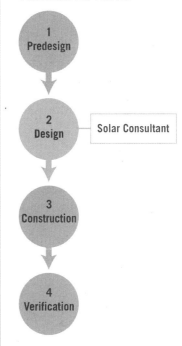

1 Predesign

2 Design — Solar Consultant

3 Construction

4 Verification

NOTES

- A project receiving points for EA 1 is not eligible for this credit, and vice versa. A project pursuing this credit must follow the prescriptive pathway and meet all the associated prerequisites in EA 2–10. Prerequisite EA 1.1 should be skipped.

DOCUMENTATION & CALCULATIONS

- Estimate the annual electricity output of the renewable electricity generating system.

- Model the annual electricity demand of the HERS Reference Home.

- Calculate the percentage of the annual reference electrical load that is met by the system.

- Calculate the number of LEED points earned, where one point is awarded for every 3% of the annual reference electrical load met by the renewable energy system.

  For example:
  Annual reference electrical load = 10,000 KWh
  Annual electricity consumption in LEED-certified home = 7,000 KWh
  Annual electricity supplied by renewable energy system = 1,800 KWh
  Percentage of annual reference electrical load supplied by renewable energy system = 1,800 / 10,000 = 18.0%
  LEED points, under EA 10 = 18.0 ÷ 3 = 6.0 points

Required | **EA 11: Residential Refrigerant Management**
EA Prerequisite 11.1: Refrigerant Charge Test

PRIMARY BENEFITS

- A properly charged coolant system helps the cooling equipment operate efficiently. A system that is overcharged or undercharged can reduce equipment longevity, capacity and efficiency.

- Reduces of ozone-depleting chemicals.

- Reduces of greenhouse gases.

STANDARDS

California Energy Commission, Appendix RD to Title 24

INTENT

Select and test air-conditioning refrigerant to ensure performance and minimize contributions to ozone depletion and global warming.

REQUIREMENTS

- Conduct and provide results of proper refrigerant charge of the air-conditioning system.

- If the home has no mechanical cooling, this measure is waived.

- If the home has a ground source heat pump, this measure is satisfied if the system is precharged and sealed.

IMPLEMENTATION

- The ideal situation would be to not use any refrigerants; therefore, planning for the best alternative is important to help in the reduction of ozone-depleting chemicals and emission of greenhouse gases.

VERIFICATION & SUBMITTALS

TRADE

- Provide refrigerant charge test results to the builder or project team leader.

PROJECT TEAM

- Include all equipment literature in the occupant's operations and maintenance manual.

- Present the refrigerant charge test results to the Green Rater.

GREEN RATER

- Visually verify the refrigerant charge test results.

DOCUMENTATION & CALCULATIONS

None

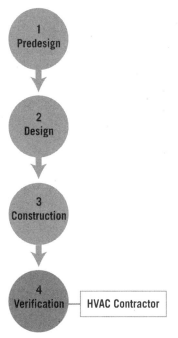

TIMELINE/TEAM

1 Predesign

2 Design

3 Construction

4 Verification — HVAC Contractor

NOTES

- If the home does not have a mechanical cooling system, the team must follow the Performance Pathway in EA 1.2.

PRIMARY BENEFITS

- HCFC refrigerants contribute to ozone depletion and global warming; therefore, switching to a non-HCFC refrigerant reduces these effects.

STANDARDS

None

INTENT

Select and test air-conditioning refrigerant to ensure performance and minimize contributions to ozone depletion and global warming.

REQUIREMENTS

- Meet one of the following:
    - Do not use refrigerants.
    - Install the HVAC system with a non-HCFC refrigerant (for example, R-410a).
    - Install an HVAC system with a refrigerant that complies with the equation from page 227 of the LEED for Homes Reference Guide, 2008.

IMPLEMENTATION

- Because HCFCs are being phased out, it is recommended that project teams make the switch to non-HCFC coolant equipment.

- Beginning in 2010, HCFCs cannot be manufactured for use in new equipment.

VERIFICATION & SUBMITTALS

TRADE

- For EA 11.2 (b) and (c), provide information related to the type of refrigerant (for example, cooling system user manuals, brochures and specifications) to the builder or project team leader.

PROJECT TEAM

- For EA 11.2 (b) and (c), present information related to the type of refrigerant (such as cooling system user manuals, brochures and specifications) to the Green Rater.

GREEN RATER

- For EA 11.2 (b) and (c), visually verify (using cooling system manuals, specifications and so on) the type of refrigerant used.

DOCUMENTATION & CALCULATIONS

- No calculations are needed if the cooling system uses R-410a. If another coolant is used, calculations will need to be performed. (See EA 11 in the LEED for Homes Reference Guide, 2008.)

TIMELINE/TEAM

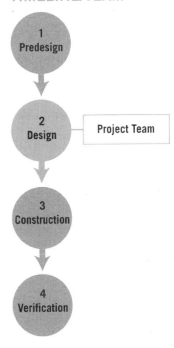

1 Predesign

2 Design — Project Team

3 Construction

4 Verification

NOTES

- This credit is available to every project, whether the performance approach (EA 1) or the prescriptive approach (EA 2–10) is used.

- If the home does not have a mechanical cooling system, the team must follow the Performance Pathway in EA 1.2.

1 What performance tests or inspections can determine the "tightness" of the home envelope and when must each one be performed?

_____

_____

2 What strategies can increase the efficiency of an HVAC system?

_____

_____

3 What strategies can increase the efficiency of a hot water system?

_____

_____

4 What credits are in the performance pathway for the EA category?

_____

_____

EA LEARNING ACTIVITIES

Contact a local **ENERGY STAR** verifier and request to shadow them on their next home verification. Note the three types of activities that they perform:

1) thermal bypass inspection;
2) visual inspection of all installed energy efficiency measures; and
3) performance tests, including overall envelope tightness and duct tightness.

ASK AROUND

Visit a home improvement store to identify energy efficient products.
Read the product literature and labels. Can you find products that meet the requirements of the prescriptive credits in the EA category?

EA Category	
HVAC	
Windows	
Hot water heater	
Refrigerator	

SITE VISIT

Visit the website of your local electric utility.
What energy efficiency incentives and services do they offer?
Rebates? If so, on what products?
Home energy audits?
Renewable energy purchase options?

INVESTIGATE

EA PRACTICE QUESTIONS

1 You have house plans that require 80% of the lighting fixtures to have the EN-ERGY STAR label. To earn credits under Advanced Lighting for Energy & Atmosphere measure 8, which of the following types of lamps would you need to install? (Select Two.)

A) ENERGY STAR labeled compact fluorescents

B) Halogens

C) LEDs

D) Low pressure sodium

E) T-12 fluorescents

2 Which energy standard is used to calculate the appropriate number of LEED points that can be earned by exceeding the performance of ENERGY STAR for Homes?

A) HERS Index

B) RESCHECK

C) REMRate

D) RESNET

3 Which of the following methods will you need to use to recognize the energy performance of the home in LEED for Homes?

A) Prescriptive Pathway

B) Performance Pathway

C) ENERGY STAR Builder Option Package Pathway

D) Your local utility's home energy efficiency program

4 An ENERGY STAR qualified home is designed to use ____% to ____% less energy than a comparable home built to the 2004 IECC standard. (Fill in the blanks.)

A) 0 to 5

B) 5 to 10

C) 10 to 15

D) 15 to 20

5 Which of the following does a Green Rater need to include in the LEED energy efficiency Prescriptive Pathway? (Select Two.)

A) Thermal bypass (insulation) inspection

B) Conduct performance tests of all appliances

C) Envelope air leakage testing with a blower door

D) Calculate an Energy Performance Score for the home

E) Document occupant behavior with regard to energy use

See Answer Key on page 268.

MATERIALS & RESOURCES

The Materials & Resources (MR) category focuses on reducing negative environmental impacts related to building materials and material waste generated during construction and operations. The MR category encourages selection of building materials that have reduced impacts associated with extraction, manufacturing, and transportation. The MR category also encourages recycling construction and building occupant waste to reduce the amount of waste that is disposed of in landfills and incinerators.

WHAT ABOUT MATERIALS & RESOURCES?

♻ Where are your building materials extracted, processed and manufactured? Why is this important?

♻ What construction and demolition debris can be reduced, reused or recycled?

♻ What would be the impact of increasing the overall recycling rate?

Photo by Jim Gallop

MATERIALS & RESOURCES

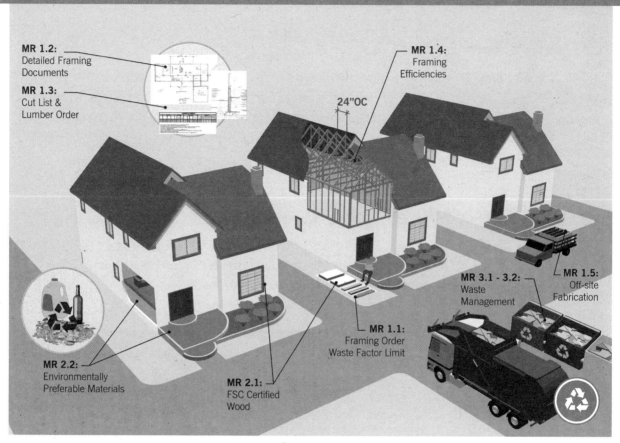

MR 1.2:
Detailed Framing Documents

MR 1.3:
Cut List & Lumber Order

MR 1.4:
Framing Efficiencies

24"OC

MR 1.5:
Off-site Fabrication

MR 3.1 - 3.2:
Waste Management

MR 1.1:
Framing Order Waste Factor Limit

MR 2.2:
Environmentally Preferable Materials

MR 2.1:
FSC Certified Wood

THE OVERVIEW

Good design decisions, particularly in the framing of homes, can significantly reduce demand for framing materials, as well as the associated waste and embedded energy. Without even changing the home design, a builder can save framing materials and reduce site waste by planning appropriately and communicating the design to the framing team through detailed framing documents and/or scopes of work.

Reclaimed (salvaged postconsumer) materials can be substituted for new materials, saving costs and reducing resource use. Recycled-content materials make use of material that would otherwise be deposited in landfills. Use of local materials supports the local economy and reduces the harmful effects of long-distance transport. Use of third party certified wood promotes good stewardship of forests and related ecosystems. Use of low-emissions materials will improve the indoor air quality in the home and reduce demand for materials with volatile organic compounds.

MATERIALS & RESOURCES

SYNERGIES

The prerequisites and credits in this section are very closely related, as the materials purchased result in human health impacts and waste generated during construction. Think of a building's material use – from the materials selected to the adhesives and caulking used to build the home – as a cycle effected by material selection and efficient purchasing, efficient use of building materials, waste reduction and waste disposal.

Develop purchasing and waste policies together, implement them at the home and track your performance. Implement efficient building techniques that reduce material use.

Think about how materials impact other aspects of the LEED for Homes Rating System. Optimizing the use of framing will reduce the amount of construction waste, and products with low emissions of volatile organic compounds (VOCs) may improve indoor air quality.

THE CREDITS

MR 1: Material-Efficient Framing	These credits require that a home be designed and built with framing strategies and techniques that reduce the use of wood.
MR 2: Environmentally Preferable Products	These credits require that a home be built without any tropical hardwood, unless it is certified by the Forest Stewardship Council, and encourage the use of environmentally preferable products, low-emissions materials and locally produced products.
MR 3: Waste Management	These credits reward projects for reducing construction waste and diverting unavoidable waste into the recycling stream.

MATERIALS & RESOURCES

KEY TERMS

adhesive	Any substance used to bond one surface to another by attachment. Adhesives include adhesive bonding primers, adhesive primers, adhesive primers for plastics and any other primer.
chain-of-custody	In forest certification, the path taken by raw materials, processed materials and products from the forest to the consumer, including all successive stages of processing, transformation, manufacturing and distribution. A chain-of-custody certificate number on invoices for nonlabeled products indicates that the certifier's guidelines for product accounting have been followed. A chain-of-custody certification is not required by distributors of a product that is individually labeled with the Forest Stewardship Council logo and manufacturer's chain-of-custody number.
composite wood	A product consisting of wood or plant particles or fibers bonded together by a synthetic resin or binder. Examples include plywood, particleboard, oriented-strand board (OSB), medium-density fiberboard (MDF) and composite door cores.
diverted waste	Debris from construction or demolition that is not sent to a landfill or incinerator. Strategies for diverting waste include reclamation, recycling and, for certain materials, mulching.
fly ash	The fine ash residue from coal combustion. Fly ash can be substituted for Portland cement, a bonding material in concrete.
Forest Stewardship Council (FSC) Certification	A seal of approval awarded to forest managers who adopt environmentally and socially responsible forest management practices and to companies that manufacture and sell products made from certified wood.
formaldehyde	A naturally occurring volatile organic compound used as a preservative. When present in high concentrations, formaldehyde can cause headaches, dizziness, mental impairment and other symptoms—and may be a carcinogen.
ladder blocking	A method of framing in which interior partition walls meet and are reinforced by exterior walls, with minimal framing.
postconsumer recycled content	Material used and then recycled by consumers, as distinguished from the recycled byproducts of manufacturing, called preconsumer (postindustrial) recycled content.
postconsumer waste	Material generated by households or by commercial, industrial and institutional facilities that can no longer be used for its intended purpose. This includes returns of materials from the distribution chain (source: ISO 14021). Examples include construction and demolition debris, materials collected through recycling programs, broken pallets (from a pallet refurbishing company, not a pallet-making company), discarded cabinetry and decking, and home maintenance waste (leaves, grass clippings, tree trimmings).

preconsumer content	Material diverted from the waste stream during the manufacturing process. Formerly known as postindustrial content. Examples include planer shavings, ply trim, sawdust, chips, bagasse, culls, trimmed materials and obsolete inventory. Excluded is reutilization of materials such as rework, regrind or scrap generated in a process and capable of being reclaimed within the same process that generated it (source: ISO 14021).
reclaimed material	Building components that have been recovered from a demolition site and are reused in their original state (that is, not recycled). Also known as salvaged or reused material.
recycled content	The weight of recycled material, including both postconsumer and preconsumer (postindustrial) material, divided by the overall weight of the assembly.
recycling	The collection, reprocessing, marketing and use of materials that were diverted or recovered from the solid waste stream.
reuse	The return of salvaged materials to use in the same or a related capacity.
salvaged material	See reclaimed material.
sustainable forestry	The practice of managing forest resources to meet the long-term forest product needs of humans while maintaining the integrity of forested landscapes and sustaining a full range of forest values—economic, social and ecological.
ureaformaldehyde	A combination of urea and formaldehyde used in some glues and adhesives, particularly in composite wood products. At room temperature, ureaformaldehyde emits formaldehyde, a toxic and possibly carcinogenic gas.
volatile organic compound (VOC)	A carbon compound that vaporizes (becomes a gas) at normal room temperatures. VOCs contribute to air pollution directly and through atmospheric photochemical reactions to produce secondary air pollutants, principally ozone and peroxyacetyl nitrate.
waste factor	The percentage of framing material ordered in excess of the estimated material needed for construction.

PRIMARY BENEFITS

- Framing lumber is a significant expense in residential housing projects, but studies have shown that a significant amount of lumber is needlessly wasted during construction. Establishing strategies to minimize assembly waste can cut down on the waste and reduce expenses.

- Less lumber in the shell reduces thermal breaks in the building shell.

STANDARDS

None

INTENT

Optimize the use of framing materials.

REQUIREMENTS

- Limit the overall estimated waste factor to 10% or less.

Table 1 from the LEED for Homes Reference Guide, 2008. Page 235. Sample Framing Order Waste Factor Calculation.

Framing component	Total cost	Waste factor	Waste cost
Random lengths	$1,000	15%	$150
Studs	$2,000	5%	$100
Beams and headers	$500	20%	$100
Roof deck	$2,000	0%	$0
Wall sheathing	$0	0%	$0
Rafters	$2,000	0%	$0
Ceiling joists	$1,500	10%	$150
Cornice work	$3,000	10%	$300
TOTAL	$12,000		$1,000
Overall waste factor (waste $ / cost $)			8.3%

IMPLEMENTATION

- Work with the architect, engineer and framer to generate an accurate estimate of the lumber needed for the project. Use this figure when ordering lumber for the home.

- The trades should be involved in the design development of the framing plan, because they will need to run wiring, piping and ducts throughout the home as the framing plan is developed.

VERIFICATION & SUBMITTALS

PROJECT TEAM

- Present calculations for the framing waste factor to the Green Rater.

GREEN RATER

- Visually verify that all calculations related to the framing waste factor have been completed.

DOCUMENTATION & CALCULATIONS

Waste factor is defined as the percentage of framing material ordered in excess of the estimated material needed for construction.

- Waste Factor = (Lumber Ordered - Lumber Needed) / Lumber Needed

TIMELINE/TEAM

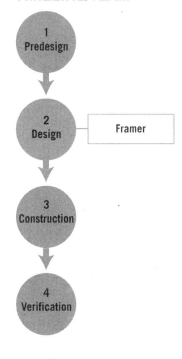

NOTES

- Optimizing the use of framing will reduce the amount of lumber waste.

PRIMARY BENEFITS

- Reduces lumber waste.
- Improves communication about framing expectations for the home.

STANDARDS

None

INTENT

Optimize the use of framing materials.

REQUIREMENTS

- Prior to construction, generate detailed framing plans or scopes of work and architectural details for use on the job site.
- Indicate on drawings the specific location, spacing and size of all framing members:
  - Floors;
  - Walls (exterior and interior);
  - Roof; and
  - Ceiling (if different from the roof).

IMPLEMENTATION

- Work with the architect/designer and, specifically, the HVAC contractor to determine the best strategy for implementing the framing plan.
- For gut-rehab projects, if 90% of the interior and exterior framing for the final LEED-certified home is salvaged or maintained, both MR 1.2 and MR 1.3 will be awarded automatically.
- There are two separate pathways to implement material-efficient framing techniques. Select either MR 1.2, 1.3 and 1.4 or MR 1.5. Points can only be counted in one pathway.

VERIFICATION & SUBMITTALS

PROJECT TEAM

- Provide detailed framing plans and/or scopes of work to the Green Rater.

GREEN RATER

- Visually verify the detailed framing plans and/or scopes of work.

DOCUMENTATION & CALCULATIONS

None

TIMELINE/TEAM

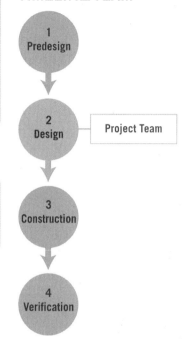

NOTES

- Detailed framing documents are used to help framers assemble a home using the most efficient strategies and techniques.

- Projects with a precut framing package (such as modular homes and kit homes) are awarded MR 1.2 and MR 1.3 automatically.

- This credit can be earned by projects with nonwood frames if the requirements are met for the relevant structural material.

PRIMARY BENEFITS

- Reduces lumber waste.

- Improves communication about framing expectations for the home.

STANDARDS

None

INTENT

Optimize the use of framing materials.

REQUIREMENTS

- Meet the requirements of MR 1.2.

- Prior to construction, create a detailed cut list and lumber order that correspond directly to the framing plans and/or scopes of work.

IMPLEMENTATION

- The framer uses the detailed framing documents to generate the cut list, which is used to place the lumber order.

VERIFICATION & SUBMITTALS

PROJECT TEAM

- Provide the detailed framing cut list and the lumber order to the Green Rater.

GREEN RATER

- Visually verify the detailed framing cut list and the lumber order.

DOCUMENTATION & CALCULATIONS

None

TIMELINE/TEAM

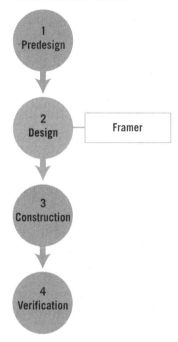

NOTES

- There are two separate pathways to implement material-efficient framing techniques. Select either MR 1.2, 1.3 and 1.4 or MR 1.5. Points can only be counted in one pathway.

- The requirements of MR 1.2 must be met to earn credit for MR 1.3.

- Projects with a precut framing package (such as modular homes and kit homes) are awarded MR 1.2 and MR 1.3 automatically.

- This credit can be earned by projects with nonwood frames if the requirements are met for the relevant structural material.

- For gut-rehab projects, if 90% of the interior and exterior framing for the final home is salvaged or maintained, both MR 1.2 and MR 1.3 will be awarded automatically.

MR 1: Material-Efficient Framing
MR Credit 1.4: Framing Efficiencies

PRIMARY BENEFITS

- Advanced framing techniques reduce the amount of lumber used to build the home without compromising its structural integrity.

STANDARDS

None

INTENT

Optimize the use of framing materials.

REQUIREMENTS

- Implement measures from the table below.

- The requirements of this credit only apply to exterior framing.

Table 4 from the LEED for Homes Reference Guide, 2008. Page 236. Efficient Framing Measures.

Measure	Points
Precut framing packages	1.0
Open-web floor trusses	1.0
Structural insulated panel (SIP) walls	1.0
SIP roof	1.0
SIP floors	1.0
Stud spacing greater than 16" o.c.	1.0
Ceiling joist spacing greater than 16" o.c.	.5
Floor joist spacing greater than 16" o.c.	.5
Roof rafter spacing greater than 16" o.c.	.5
Implement any two of the following: • Size headers for actual loads • Use ladder blocking or drywall clips • Use 2-stud corners	.5

Exemplary Performance: Projects that implement advanced framing measures worth more than three points can take credit for the additional measures, to be counted under ID 3, Innovative or Regional Design.

IMPLEMENTATION

- Advanced framing techniques need to be incorporated early in the planning process.

- Alternative measures not listed on Table 2 on page 236 of the LEED for Homes Reference Guide, 2008, may be eligible to earn points if they save comparable amounts of framing material. A formal Credit Interpretation Request with full justification of any alternative measure's potential savings must be submitted to USGBC by the LEED for Homes Provider.

IMPLEMENTATION, CONTINUED

- Advanced framing techniques have been around for many years, but they are rarely incorporated into projects. Framing crews often default to standard framing techniques, so the implementation of a detailed framing strategy and follow-up in the field is critical.

VERIFICATION & SUBMITTALS

GREEN RATER

- Visually verify the use of advanced framing measures in the home.

DOCUMENTATION & CALCULATIONS

None

TIMELINE/TEAM

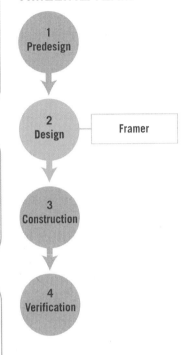

NOTES

- There are two separate pathways to implement material-efficient framing techniques. Select either MR 1.2, 1.3 and 1.4 or MR 1.5. Points can only be counted in one pathway.

- If during the examination of MR 1.5 the project team decides to use only panelized walls, then the project team can earn two points under MR 1.4.

PRIMARY BENEFITS

- These techniques are more expensive than standard on-site framing, but they allow the home to be assembled on-site more quickly than with normal framing, reducing assembly expenses reducing the amount of wood used for framing.

- The home is built in factory settings, allowing less chance of weather effects during construction, and greater quality control over assembly.

STANDARDS

None

INTENT

Optimize the use of framing materials.

REQUIREMENTS

- Choose one of the following to implement:
  - ○ Panelized construction:
    - Preframed wall, roof and floor components are delivered to the job site (points are awarded only if the preframed components are assembled off-site).
  - ○ Modular, prefabricated construction:
    - All principal building sections are delivered to the job site as prefabricated modules.

IMPLEMENTATION

- Implementing panelized or prefabricated strategies takes extra planning to ensure that all relevant construction issues have been dealt with, such as penetrations, wiring, plumbing and ducting.

VERIFICATION & SUBMITTALS

GREEN RATER

- Visually verify the use of panelized or modular, prefabricated construction on-site.

DOCUMENTATION & CALCULATIONS

None

TIMELINE/TEAM

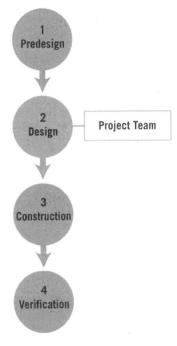

1
Predesign

2
Design — Project Team

3
Construction

4
Verification

NOTES

- There are two separate pathways to implement material-efficient framing techniques. Select either MR 1.2, 1.3 and 1.4 or MR 1.5. Points can only be counted in one pathway.

- These strategies are in the early development phase for residential construction; thus, they are not widely available.

- If the project team decides to use only panelized walls, the two points can be awarded under MR 1.4.

 **Required** | # MR 2: Environmentally Preferable Products
MR Prerequisite 2.1: FSC-Certified Tropical Woods

PRIMARY BENEFITS

- Reduces impact on rainforests.
- Increases exposure for and awareness of FSC-certified wood.

STANDARDS

None

INTENT

Increase demand for environmentally preferable products and products or building components that are extracted, processed and manufactured within the region.

REQUIREMENTS

- Meet the following requirements:
  - ○ Provide all wood product suppliers with a notice regarding tropical wood that contains:
    - A statement that the builder prefers to purchase tropical wood only if it is FSC-certified;
    - A request that the country of origin be identified for each wood product supplied;
    - A request for a list of FSC-certified wood products that the supplier can provide.
  - ○ If tropical wood is to be used, it must be FSC-certified.
  - ○ Reused or reclaimed tropical hardwood materials are exempt from the FSC-certified requirement.

IMPLEMENTATION

- The notice needs to be generated before construction and provided to all wood product vendors for the project.

VERIFICATION & SUBMITTALS

PROJECT TEAM

- Provide the required notice to all wood products suppliers.

- Present the wood supplier notice to the Green Rater.

- Sign an Accountability Form confirming that no tropical woods were used except those that were FSC-certified or reclaimed.

GREEN RATER

- Visually verify that the wood supplier notice has been provided to vendors and that it meets the stated requirements.

- Verify that the Accountability Form has been signed by the responsible party.

DOCUMENTATION & CALCULATIONS

- Notice to vendors.

TIMELINE/TEAM

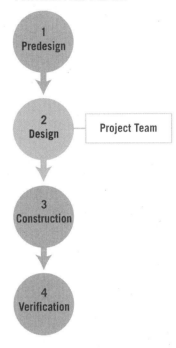

1 Predesign

2 Design — Project Team

3 Construction

4 Verification

NOTES

- FSC (Forest Stewardship Council) certified wood helps ensure that environmentally and socially responsible forestry practices have been implemented by companies that manufacture and sell wood building products.

- A species of wood is considered tropical if it is grown in a country that lies between the Tropics of Cancer and Capricorn.

PRIMARY BENEFITS

- Reduces environmental impact.

STANDARDS

Green Seal Standards GS-11 and GS-43

South Coast Air Quality Management District Rule 1113, Standard for Architectural Coatings

INTENT

Increase demand for environmentally preferable products and products or building components that are extracted, processed and manufactured within the region.

REQUIREMENTS

- Incorporate into the home building products that meet one or more of the criteria on the Environmentally Preferable Products list from page 248 of the LEED for Homes Reference Guide, 2008. Each product that meets the criteria of MR 2.2 (a), environmentally preferable products; MR 2.2 (b), low emissions; and MR 2.2 (c), local production, can earn points in each criterion.

  ○ Environmentally preferable products (0.5 point per component):
    - Recycled-content products must contain 25% postconsumer content or 50% postindustrial (preconsumer) content.

  AND/OR

  ○ Low emissions (0.5 point per component):
    - Meet the requirements listed in Tables 2 and 3 on pages 249 and 250 of the LEED for Homes Reference Guide, 2008.

  AND/OR

  ○ Local production (0.5 point per component):
    - Products must be (entire life cycle) extracted, harvested, processed and manufactured within 500 miles of the home.

Exemplary Performance: Projects that use more than 16 of the options in Table 1 on page 248 of the LEED for Homes Reference Guide, 2008 and can earn more than the maximum eight points can earn additional points at 0.5 point per additional measure to be counted under ID 3. The maximum allowable exemplary performance points are four.

IMPLEMENTATION

- Early planning is necessary to ensure that all opportunities for implementation of products into the home can be accomplished. Ensure that the project superintendent understands what products are to be installed and why they have been selected.

VERIFICATION & SUBMITTALS

PROJECT TEAM

- Present any relevant product stamps, certification labels, web links, and/or literature to the Green Rater as needed to demonstrate that the credit requirements were met.

- Sign an Accountability Form to indicate that each product being counted in this credit represents the required minimum percentage of the applicable component.

GREEN RATER

- Visually verify (using product stamps, labels, web links and/or literature, as needed) that all products counted in this credit meet the relevant requirements and were used in the project.

- Verify that an Accountability Form has been signed by the responsible party.

DOCUMENTATION & CALCULATIONS

- Detailed calculations are not required for each component. Approximations are acceptable, and no calculation needs to be performed if the component in its entirety meets the requirement.

- To earn 0.5 point, at least 90% of a given component by weight or volume must meet the requirements for environmentally preferable products, low emissions or local production. This can be achieved with multiple products.

  Example: If 70% of countertops are FSC wood and 20% of countertops are reclaimed wood, 20% + 70% = 90%, and the project will earn 0.5 point.

  - Exceptions to the 90% requirement:
    - 45% of floor area (square feet is the metric), and
    - 90% of floor area (square feet is the metric).

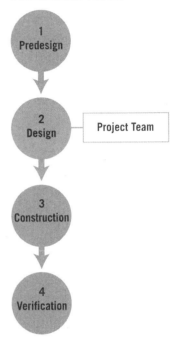

TIMELINE/TEAM

1. Predesign
2. Design — Project Team
3. Construction
4. Verification

NOTES

- Local production means that 90% of the product by weight or volume must be extracted, harvested, processed and manufactured within 500 miles of the home. Assembly of the product within 500 miles of the home does not qualify by itself.

- Cradle-to-Cradle (C2C) certification is an acceptable alternative for any component in the environmentally preferable products column. Credit cannot be granted, however, for being C2C-certified and also meeting the existing criteria (such as recycled content, reclaimed content or FSC-certified).

PRIMARY BENEFITS

- Reduces of waste generated.
- Reduces of waste that goes to landfills.
- Increases rate of recycling of useful materials.

STANDARDS

None

INTENT

Reduce waste generation to a level below the industry norm.

REQUIREMENTS

- Complete the following tasks:

    ○ Investigate and document the local options for diversion of all waste streams.

    ○ Document the diversion rate for construction waste.

    ○ Record the diversion rate for land clearing and/or demolition separately from the rate for new construction, if applicable.

Exemplary Performance: Projects that can demonstrate that no waste was created or that 100% of the waste was diverted can earn an additional 0.5 point, to be counted under ID 3.

IMPLEMENTATION

- Training the construction staff is key to accomplishing a high rate of recycling. Choices need to be made on what to do with waste, and if the construction staff is not involved in this effort, problems will occur.

- The waste hauler needs to be involved early in the construction of the home to ensure that the recycling of waste can take place. Setting up separate bins for each type of waste product that can be recycled works best.

- Wood scraps that are incinerated, even if for power generation, cannot be counted as diverted and must be counted as land filled materials.

- The waste hauler and construction crews will make or break the accomplishment of this measure.

MR 3: Waste Management. MR Prerequisite 3.1: Construction Waste Management Planning

Exemplary Performance

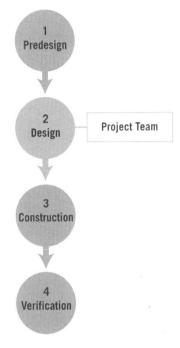

VERIFICATION & SUBMITTALS

PROJECT TEAM

- Present documentation of local waste diversion options to the Green Rater.

- Present calculations to the Green Rater demonstrating construction waste diversion rate, using documentation from the waste management company.

GREEN RATER

- Verify documentation of local waste diversion options.

- Verify calculations of construction waste diversion rate.

DOCUMENTATION & CALCULATIONS

- Document the waste totals with receipts from the waste hauling company, using the LEED for Homes Reference Guide, 2008 Edition, page 264, Table 2.

- Calculate the amounts of waste reduction and waste diversion.

- Reduced construction waste:

  - Step 1: Calculate the net construction waste in weight or volume:
    - Net Waste = Waste Sent to Landfill + Waste Incinerated
    OR
    - Net Waste = Total Waste Hauled - (Material Reclaimed + Material Recycled)
  - Step 2: Calculate the waste rate from construction:
    - Waste Rate (pounds/square foot) = Net Waste / Home Size
    OR
    - Waste Rate (cubic yards /1,000 square feet) = Net Waste / Home Size / 1,000

- Increased waste diversion:

  - Step 1: Calculate the amount of waste diverted from landfills or incinerators:
    - Waste Diverted = Total Waste Hauled – (Waste Sent to Landfill + Waste Incinerated)
    OR
    - Waste Diverted = Material Reclaimed + Material Recycled
  - Step 2: Calculate the percentage of waste diverted from the landfill or incinerator:
    - Waste Diverted (%) = Waste Diverted / Total Waste Hauled

TIMELINE/TEAM

1 Predesign

2 Design — Project Team

3 Construction

4 Verification

NOTES

- Land clearing and demolition waste should not be counted in the calculation.

MR 3: Waste Management
MR Credit 3.2: Construction Waste Reduction

PRIMARY BENEFITS

- Reduces of waste generated.

- Reduces of waste that goes to landfills.

- Increases rate of recycling of useful materials.

STANDARDS

None

INTENT

Reduce waste generation to a level below the industry norm.

REQUIREMENTS

- Reduce waste or divert waste from landfills and incinerators. Use either of two options:

  o Reduced construction waste:
    - Generate 2.5 pounds, or 0.016 cubic yards, or less per square foot of building floor area.

  o Increased waste diversion:
    - Divert 25% or more of the total materials taken off the construction site from landfills or incinerators.

Exemplary Performance: Projects that can demonstrate that no waste was created or that 100% of the waste was diverted can earn an additional 0.5 point, to be counted under ID 3.

IMPLEMENTATION

- Training the construction staff is key to accomplishing a high rate of recycling. Choices need to be made on what to do with waste, and if the construction staff is not involved in this effort, problems will occur.

- The waste hauler needs to be involved early in the construction of the home to ensure that the recycling of waste can take place. Setting up separate bins for each type of waste product that can be recycled works best.

- Wood waste that is diverted from landfills but ends up being used as fuel to generate power is not considered to be diverted from a landfill. Add this to the amount of waste that goes to a landfill.

VERIFICATION & SUBMITTALS

PROJECT TEAM

- Present calculations to the Green Rater demonstrating average waste in pounds or cubic yards per square foot for the project, using documentation from the waste management company.

- Present calculations to the Green Rater demonstrating construction waste diversion rates, using documentation from the waste management company.

GREEN RATER

- Verify the calculations of average construction waste.

- Verify the calculations of the construction waste diversion rate.

DOCUMENTATION & CALCULATIONS

- Use same calculation as MR 3.1.

TIMELINE/TEAM

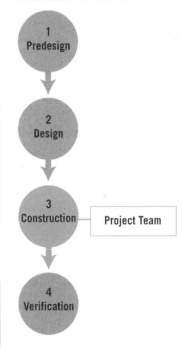

NOTES

- Land clearing and demolition waste should not be counted in the calculation.

1 Name the primary strategies that can help project teams earn credit for waste reduction and diversion.

_____

_____

2 What are the definitions of the following terms in relation to environmentally preferable products: a) preconsumer, b) postindustrial, c) postconsumer?

_____

_____

3 How is the term "locally-produced product" defined?

_____

_____

4 What are four types of products that can have high Volatile Organic Compounds (VOC) content?

_____

_____

Investigate the resources in your area for used, reclaimed and recycled building materials. Record what you find.

INVESTIGATE

Outline the procedure you will take to monitor, collect, and promote waste management planning on a site.

Step	Description
Monitor	
Collect	
Promote	

PUT IT IN PRACTICE

Conduct an informational interview with a green builder in your area. Ask if they can share documentation with you that shows information about FSC-certified tropical wood or country of origin.

ASK AROUND

1 What attributes do qualifying environmentally preferable materials have?

A) Recycled or reclaimed content

B) High emissions of volatile organic compounds (VOCs)

C) The product was manufactured 100 miles from where it was extracted

D) Rainforest Alliance-certified wood

2 Which of the following strategies can be incorporated into your design to frame efficiently?

A) Use structural insulated panels (SIPs).

B) Use fewer nails and/or screws.

C) Use renewable energy sources for powered equipment.

D) Use concrete mixed with fly ash.

3 What is the best strategy for reducing your overall framing waste factor?

A) Incorporate extra wood into the framing of the home.

B) Order only the amount that you need.

C) Create a detailed framing order and cut list.

D) Donate extra wood to your local Habitat for Humanity.

4 A product was harvested 300 miles away from the project site and then moved 300 miles further away to be processed. After the product was purchased, it traveled an additional 100 miles to the project site.

According to MR 2.2, Environmentally Preferable Product, select the correct statement.

A) The project would earn ½ point because it was harvested within 500 miles of the project.

B) The product can qualify if it contains a minimum of 25% postconsumer recycled content.

C) The product is composed of 90% raw material, by weight or volume.

D) The product does not qualify to earn the Local Production point.

5 An application of Construction Waste Reduction is _____?

A) framing lumber that is recycled and then incinerated.

B) framing lumber that is chipped for mulch.

C) scrap metal that goes to the landfill.

D) cardboard that is used to protect the finished floor of a home and thrown away.

See Answer Key on page 269.

INDOOR ENVIRONMENTAL QUALITY

The Indoor Environmental Quality (EQ) category addresses the critical effects building performance has on occupants and users. This category aims at improving ventilation, managing air contaminants, improving occupant comfort and allowing for safer environments for building operators and occupants.

WHAT ABOUT INDOOR ENVIRONMENTAL QUALITY?

How clean is the air that we breathe? How could it be improved?

What are common sources of indoor air contaminants within the home?

Why is it important to control indoor moisture?

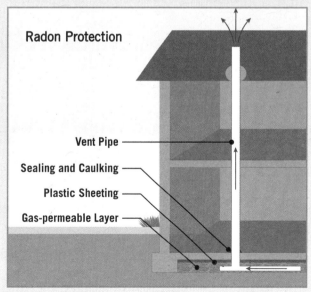

Radon Protection

Vent Pipe

Sealing and Caulking

Plastic Sheeting

Gas-permeable Layer

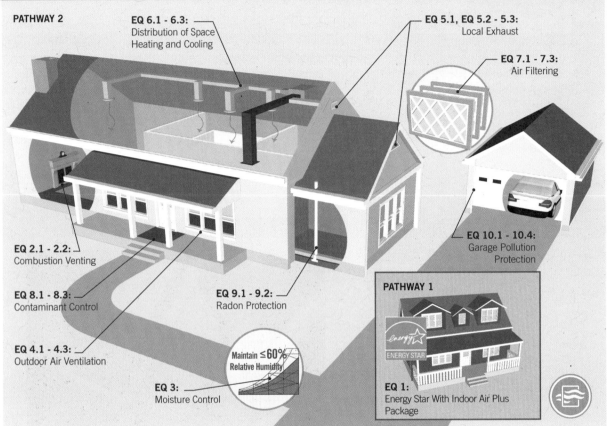

PATHWAY 2

EQ 6.1 - 6.3:
Distribution of Space
Heating and Cooling

EQ 5.1, EQ 5.2 - 5.3:
Local Exhaust

EQ 7.1 - 7.3:
Air Filtering

EQ 10.1 - 10.4:
Garage Pollution
Protection

EQ 2.1 - 2.2:
Combustion Venting

EQ 8.1 - 8.3:
Contaminant Control

EQ 9.1 - 9.2:
Radon Protection

PATHWAY 1

EQ 4.1 - 4.3:
Outdoor Air Ventilation

Maintain ≤60%
Relative Humidity

EQ 3:
Moisture Control

EQ 1:
Energy Star With Indoor Air Plus
Package

THE OVERVIEW

Over the past 20 years, research and experience have improved our understanding of what is involved in attaining high indoor environmental quality and revealed manufacturing and construction practices that can prevent problems from arising. Preventing indoor air quality problems is generally much less expensive than identifying and solving them after they occur. Generally, there are three types of strategies: source removal, source control and dilution.

The Indoor Environmental Quality category encourages builders to prevent air pollution and improve air quality and comfort in the homes they build.

Since the release in 1987 of EPA reports that designated indoor air pollution as a top environmental risk to public heath, assessing and managing indoor pollutants have become the focus of integrated governmental and private efforts. In addition to health and liability concerns, productivity gains are driving improvements in indoor environmental quality. Employees' salaries are a significant cost in any commercial building, so it makes good business sense to keep staff healthy, alert, and productive.

INDOOR ENVIRONMENTAL QUALITY

SYNERGIES

The prerequisites and credits in this category are designed to help create a home that incorporates strategies that reduce pollutant exposure to humans during the construction of the home through to occupancy of the home by the home buyer.

These strategies focus on a three step process. It starts out with investigating and then installing materials and equipment that can reduce impacts on human health. The second step focuses on selection and implementation of strategies that provide for adequate ventilation to dilute any pollutants that are in the home. The third step looks at ways to provide filtration that removes pollutants from the indoor air of the home. These three steps help improve the indoor air quality for the construction workers and the occupants of the home.

Also, think about how the measures within this category impact others in the LEED for Homes Rating System: Improved foundation, exterior walls, and roof water management should be addressed in the durability inspection checklist (ID 2). In hot and humid climates, dehumidification can reduce the energy demands associated with air-conditioning (EA 1, EA 6). Exhaust fans (EA 5.1) can simultaneously provide the outdoor air ventilation system for the home. Finally, products with low VOC emissions (MR 2) greatly benefit indoor air quality.

INDOOR ENVIRONMENTAL QUALITY

EQ

THE CREDITS

There are two pathways to achieve these credits:

Pathway 1 with ENERGY STAR	
EQ 1: ENERGY STAR with Indoor Air Package	This program is designed to encourage healthier indoor air quality in new homes. It implements a comprehensive set of measures for ventilation, source control and source removal.

OR

Pathway 2 with Prescriptive Approach	
EQ 2: Combustion Venting	These credits require the implementation of basic strategies that reduce exposure of homeowners to toxic combustion exhaust gases. The credit also rewards homes that implement better and/or best practices that reduce exposure of homeowners to toxic combustion exhaust gases.
EQ 3: Moisture Control	This credit rewards projects that manage the moisture balance in the home during both summer and winter conditions.
EQ 4: Outdoor Air Ventilation	These credits require the implementation of basic outdoor air ventilation strategies that improve the air quality of the home. The credit also rewards homes that incorporate products that are energy-efficient and provide superior ventilation. This section also rewards homes that test the performance of the ventilation equipment.
EQ 5: Local Exhaust	These credits require the implementation of basic localized exhaust strategies that improve the air quality of the home. They also reward homes that incorporate products that are energy-efficient and provide superior exhaust. This section also rewards homes that test the performance of the exhaust equipment.
EQ 6: Distribution Systems	These credits ensure that each room in the home has adequate heating and cooling through the incorporation of design calculations and implementation of properly sized equipment. It also rewards homes that test the performance of the air distribution system.
EQ 7: Air Filtering	This credit is aimed at improving the effectiveness of air filters in furnaces, air handlers and ventilation systems.
EQ 8: Contaminant Control	These credits reward controlling contaminants and improving indoor air quality during construction and homeowner occupancy of the home.
EQ 9: Radon Protection	These credits are aimed at reducing homeowner exposure to radon gases through the implementation of radon-resistant construction techniques.
EQ 10: Garage Pollutant Protection	These credits ensure that strategies are implemented to reduce exposure of homeowners to garage pollutants.

KEY TERMS

balancing damper	An adjustable plate that regulates airflow within ducts.
central vacuum system	A network of tubing with inlets throughout the home designed to remove dust and debris to a remote receptacle. A central vacuum system is more efficient than a traditional vacuum cleaner.
closed combustion	A design for furnaces and water heaters in which the supply air is ducted from the outside and exhaust gases are ducted to the outdoors. All elements of the system are sealed to prevent combustion exhaust from leaking into the home.
combustion exhaust gases	The most common gases resulting from fossil fuel combustion, including carbon dioxide, carbon monoxide, sulfur dioxide and nitrogen oxides. These gases pose health hazards at high concentrations.
ENERGY STAR with Indoor airPLUS (IAP)	A certification program that recognizes homes with systems that ensure high standards of indoor air quality.
hydronic system	A heating or cooling system that uses circulating water as the heat-transfer medium, such as a boiler with hot water circulated through radiators.
minimum efficiency reporting value (MERV)	The effectiveness of a mechanical air filter based on the number and size of the particles that pass through it under normal conditions. The higher the rating, the more effective the filter.
power-vented exhaust	The use of an active fan system to pull combustion gases out of the home. Combustion equipment with power venting can use indoor air as the combustion supply air.
radon	A radioactive gas that naturally vents from the ground. Not all homes have problems with radon. High levels of radon are known to be carcinogenic.
walk-off mat	An exterior pad or grate designed to trap dust and debris.

13 Points | **EQ 1: ENERGY STAR with Indoor Air Package**
EQ Credit 1: ENERGY STAR with Indoor Air Package

PRIMARY BENEFITS

- Improves air quality for the home.

- Improves durability of many components of the home.

STANDARDS

EPA's Indoor airPLUS program

INTENT

Improve the overall quality of a home's indoor environment by installing an approved bundle of air quality measures.

REQUIREMENTS

- Complete all the requirements of the U.S. Environmental Protection Agency's ENERGY STAR with Indoor airPLUS program (previously named Indoor Air Package).

IMPLEMENTATION

- The EPA Indoor airPLUS program is a holistic air quality program.

- This program requires verification and documentation by an accredited third party trained by EPA.

VERIFICATION & SUBMITTALS

PROJECT TEAM

● Present ENERGY STAR with Indoor airPLUS certification to the Green Rater.

GREEN RATER

● Verify that ENERGY STAR with Indoor airPLUS certification has been achieved.

DOCUMENTATION & CALCULATIONS

None

TIMELINE/TEAM

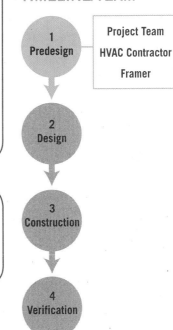

NOTES

● A project receiving points for this credit may skip the prerequisites in EQ2–10 and is not eligible to earn points in EQ 2.2, 3, 4.3, 6, 8.1, 8.3, 9 and 10.

● Achieving the measures in the Indoor airPLUS program may qualify a home to receive points in other categories of the LEED for Homes Rating System.

PRIMARY BENEFITS

- Implementing a strategy to reduce exposure to combustion byproducts can lead to improved indoor air quality.

STANDARDS

IECC-2007 Climate Zones

INTENT

Minimize the leakage of combustion gases into the occupied spaces of the home.

REQUIREMENTS

- Meet all of the following requirements:
  - No unvented combustion appliances.
  - Carbon monoxide (CO) monitor installed on each floor of the home (or each floor of each unit, for multifamily projects). Carbon monoxide detectors are required to be installed in all homes, even if they do not have any combustion-generating products in the home.
  - No fireplace installed, OR all fireplaces and wood stoves must have doors.
  - Space and water heating that involves combustion must meet one of the following:
    - Closed combustion;
    - Power-vented exhaust;
    - Located in detached or open-air facility; or
    - No space- or water-heating equipment with combustion.
  - Space heating systems located in IECC-2007 Climate Zone 1 or 2 are exempt from this measure.

IMPLEMENTATION

- Early involvement of the builder and client will help ensure that the measures are accomplished.

VERIFICATION & SUBMITTALS

GREEN RATER

- Visually verify that all requirements of the prerequisite have been met.

DOCUMENTATION & CALCULATIONS

- Homes with a wood-burning stove or fireplace must pass a back-draft potential test. This calculation requires a blower door test.

TIMELINE/TEAM

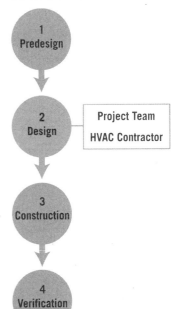

1 Predesign

2 Design — Project Team / HVAC Contractor

3 Construction

4 Verification

NOTES

None

PRIMARY BENEFITS

- Implementing a strategy to reduce exposure to combustion byproducts can lead to improved indoor air quality.

STANDARDS

IECC-2007 Climate Zones

INTENT

Minimize the leakage of combustion gases into the occupied spaces of the home.

REQUIREMENTS

Install no fireplace or wood stove, or design and install a fireplace or wood stove according to table below.

Table 1 from the LEED for Homes Reference Guide, 2008. Page 278. Fireplace and Stove Combustion-Venting Requirements.

Fireplace or stove	Enhanced combustion-venting measures	
	Better practice (1 point)	Best practice (2 points)
None	See "best practice".	Granted automatically.
Masonry wood-burning fireplace	Install masonry heater as defined by American Society for Testing and Materials Standard E-1602 and International Building Code 2112.1.	Meet requirement for "better practice", and conduct back-draft potential test to ensure $\Delta P \leq 5$ Pascals (see "Conducting a Back-Draft Potential Test" below).
Factory-built wood-burning fireplace	Install equipment listed by approved safety testing facility (e.g., UL, CSA, ETL) that either is EPA certified or meets the following: equipment with catalytic combustor must emit less than 4.1 g/hr of particulate matter, and equipment without catalytic combustor must emit less than 7.5 g/hr of particulate matter.	Meet requirement for better practice, and conduct back-draft potential test to ensure $\Delta P \leq 5$ Pascals (see "Conducting a Back-DraftPotential Test" below).
Woodstove and fireplace insert	Install equipment listed by approved safety testing facility that either is EPA certified or meets following requirement: equipment with catalytic combustor must emit less than 4.1 g/hr of particulate matter, and equipment without catalytic combustor must emit less than 7.5 g/hr of particulate matter.	Meet requirement for better practice, and conduct back-draft potential test to ensure $\Delta P \leq 5$ Pascals (see "Conducting a Back-Draft Potential Test" below).
Natural gas, propane, or alcohol stove	Install equipment listed by approved safety testing facility that is power-vented or direct-vented and has permanently fixed glass front or gasketed door.	Meet requirement for better practice, and include electronic (not standing) pilot.
Pellet stove	Install equipment that is either EPA certified or listed by approved safety testing facility to have met requirements of ASTM E 1509-04, "Standard Specification for Room Heaters, Pellet Fuel-Burning Type."	Meet requirement for better practice, and include power venting or direct venting.

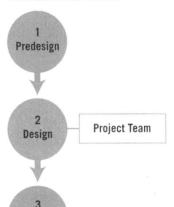

IMPLEMENTATION

- Evaluate all combustion-producing products in the home and develop a holistic strategy to manage or eliminate all of the sources of combustion byproducts.

VERIFICATION & SUBMITTALS

PROJECT TEAM

- Present any fireplace or stove equipment literature to the Green Rater for visual inspection.

- Include fireplace or stove equipment literature in the occupant's operations and maintenance manual.

GREEN RATER

- Visually verify that all requirements of the prerequisite have been met.

- Visually verify that all applicable standards and certifications have been met:

  - Check the safety listing in the appliance user manual.
  - Check EPA certification on the EPA website.

- For best practices with a wood-burning stove or fireplace, visually verify that back-draft calculations are completed.

- Visually verify all applicable equipment in the home.

DOCUMENTATION & CALCULATIONS

- Homes with a wood-burning stove or fireplace must pass a back-draft potential test. This calculation requires a blower door test.

TIMELINE/TEAM

1 Predesign

2 Design — Project Team

3 Construction

4 Verification

NOTES

- A project receiving points for EQ 1 is not eligible to earn points in EQ 2.2. A project pursuing EQ 2.2 must meet all the prerequisites in EQ 2–10.

PRIMARY BENEFITS

- Dehumidification of indoor air can lead to improved comfort and reduced energy consumption.

STANDARDS

ASHRAE Handbook of Fundamentals for moisture loads

INTENT

Control indoor moisture levels to provide comfort, reduce the risk of mold and increase the durability of the home.

REQUIREMENTS

- Install dehumidification equipment with sufficient latent capacity to maintain relative humidity at or below 60%. Meet one of the following:

  o Additional dehumidification system; or

  o Central HVAC system equipped with additional controls to operate in dehumidification mode.

- The project team needs to prove that an active dehumidification system is needed before the point will be awarded for the installation of a dehumidification system.

IMPLEMENTATION

- The HVAC contractor needs to determine the moisture load for the home and evaluate it with the ASHRAE Handbook of Fundamentals to determine whether an active dehumidification system needs to be installed.

VERIFICATION & SUBMITTALS

TRADE

- Provide any equipment literature (such as user manuals, brochures and specifications) to the builder or project team leader.

- Provide calculations of latent capacity to the builder or project team leader.

PROJECT TEAM

- Present calculations of latent capacity to the Green Rater.

- Include dehumidification equipment literature in the occupant's operations and maintenance manual.

GREEN RATER

- Visually verify that all calculations related to latent capacity are completed.

- Visually verify all applicable equipment in the home.

TIMELINE/TEAM

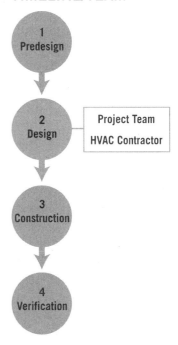

1 Predesign

2 Design — Project Team / HVAC Contractor

3 Construction

4 Verification

DOCUMENTATION & CALCULATIONS

- An engineer or HVAC contractor should use infiltration and ventilation rates to calculate the amount of moisture removed in winter and added in summer. This is used to determine whether active moisture control measures are needed.

NOTES

- A project receiving points for EQ 1 is not eligible to earn points in EQ 3. A project pursuing EQ 3 must meet all the prerequisites in EQ 2–10.

PRIMARY BENEFITS

- Improves indoor air quality.
- Reduces moisture loads.

STANDARDS

Equation 4.2 of ASHRAE Standard 62.2-2007

INTENT

Reduce occupant exposure to indoor pollutants by ventilating with outdoor air.

REQUIREMENTS

Design and install a whole-building ventilation system that complies with ASHRAE Standard 62.2-2007. The HVAC contractor should review and follow the requirements of ASHRAE Standard 62.2-2007, Sections 4 and 7. Meet one of the following:

- Exempted if located in a climate with fewer than 4,500 infiltration degree-days. Operable windows need to be incorporated as part of this strategy.

- Continuous ventilation: Must meet minimum airflow requirements for continuous ventilation systems from ASHRAE Standard 62.2-2007.

- Intermittent ventilation: Use Equation 4.2 of ASHRAE Standard 62.2-2007 to demonstrate compliance.

- Passive ventilation: System must be approved and verified by a licensed HVAC engineer.

IMPLEMENTATION

- Exhaust systems need to be incorporated in most homes to ensure that adequate ventilation exists. Using ASHRAE Standard 62.2 helps address various strategies that can be incorporated into the home.

VERIFICATION & SUBMITTALS

TRADE

- For EQ 4.1 (b) and (c), provide calculations to the builder or project team leader demonstrating that the ventilation system is designed to meet the requirements.

- For EQ 4.1 (b), (c) and (d), sign an Accountability Form to indicate that the system is installed according to the design specifications.

- Deliver any ventilation equipment literature (such as user manuals, brochures and specifications) to the builder or project team leader.

PROJECT TEAM

- For EQ 4.1 (b) and (c), present calculations to the Green Rater demonstrating that the ventilation system is designed to meet the requirements.

- Include equipment literature in the occupant's operations and maintenance manual.

GREEN RATER

- For EQ 4.1 (b) and (c), visually verify that all calculations related to outdoor air ventilation are completed.

- For EQ 4.1 (b), (c) and (d), verify that an Accountability Form has been signed by the responsible party.

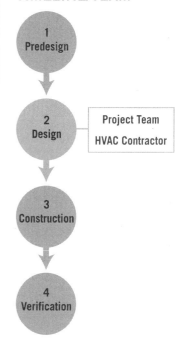

TIMELINE/TEAM

1 Predesign

2 Design — Project Team / HVAC Contractor

3 Construction

4 Verification

NOTES

- As homes are built to be tighter and infiltration air is reduced, controlled ventilation needs to be introduced to provide fresh air to the occupants.

- When the HVAC and heating and cooling system is being designed (EA 5, 6: EQ 4, 6) EQ 10.1 must be taken into consideration.

DOCUMENTATION & CALCULATIONS

- The number of infiltration degree-days is equal to the sum of cooling degree-days and heating degree-days.

2 Points

EQ 4: Outdoor Air Ventilation
EQ Credit 4.2: Enhanced Outdoor Air Ventilation

PRIMARY BENEFITS

- Provides a whole-house solution to indoor air ventilation.

- Improves air quality.

- Reduces cost to condition indoor air.

STANDARDS

ASHRAE 62.2-2007

INTENT

Reduce occupant exposure to indoor pollutants by ventilating with outdoor air.

REQUIREMENTS

Meet one of the following:

- In climates with fewer than 4,500 infiltration degree-days, install an active ventilation system that complies with ASHRAE 62.2-2007.

  OR

- Install a system that provides heat transfer between the incoming outdoor air stream and the exhaust air stream, such as a heat-recovery ventilator (HRV) or an energy-recovery ventilator (ERV).

IMPLEMENTATION

- A project receiving points for EQ 1 is not eligible to earn points for EQ 4.3, but may earn points for EQ 4.2.

- Determine the need for indoor air exhaust and evaluate whether using a heat- or energy-recovery ventilator can meet those needs effectively.

VERIFICATION & SUBMITTALS

TRADE

- For 4.2 (a), provide calculations to the builder or project team leader demonstrating that the ventilation system is designed to meet the requirements.

- For 4.2 (a), sign an Accountability Form to indicate that the system has been installed according to the design specifications.

- Provide any equipment literature (such as user manuals, brochures and specifications) to the builder or project team leader.

PROJECT TEAM

- For 4.2 (a), present calculations to the Green Rater demonstrating that the ventilation system is designed to meet the requirements.

- Include any ventilation system equipment literature in the occupant's operations and maintenance manual.

GREEN RATER

- For 4.2 (a), visually verify that all calculations related to outdoor air ventilation have been completed.

- For 4.2 (a), verify that an Accountability Form has been signed by the responsible party.

- Visually verify all applicable equipment in the home.

DOCUMENTATION & CALCULATIONS

- Equations 4.1 (a) and 4.1 (b) in ASHRAE 62.2-2007, Section 4.

TIMELINE/TEAM

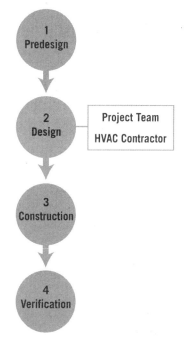

NOTES

- A heat- or energy-recovery ventilator captures the heat or coolness of the exhaust air and returns it to the incoming air stream, thus preconditioning the incoming air and reducing the energy used to condition the incoming air.

- A home that uses a radiant floor-heating system will typically benefit from the installation of a heat-recovery system.

- The heat-recovery system must be listed by a certified testing lab (such as UL or ETL).

- When the HVAC and heating and cooling system is being designed (EA 5, 6: EQ 4, 6) EQ 10.1 must be taken into consideration.

PRIMARY BENEFITS

- Third-party testing helps ensure that the installed system is functioning as designed.

STANDARDS

ASHRAE 62.2-2007

INTENT

Reduce occupant exposure to indoor pollutants by ventilating with outdoor air.

REQUIREMENTS

- Have a third party test the flow rate of air brought into the home.

- Verify that the requirements of ASHRAE 62.2-2007 are met.

- In exhaust-only ventilation systems, install exhaust ducts according to Table 7.1 of ASHRAE Standard 62.2-2007:
  - Test the flow rate out of the home;
    OR
  - Conduct airflow tests to ensure a back pressure of ≤ 0.20 inches w.c.

IMPLEMENTATION

- Have a third party test the performance of the ventilation system.

VERIFICATION & SUBMITTALS

GREEN RATER

- Test the outdoor ventilation airflow into the home and verify that it meets the requirements.

DOCUMENTATION & CALCULATIONS

- The third-party tester will take the results of the test and determine whether they meet the requirements of ASHRAE 62.2-2007.

TIMELINE/TEAM

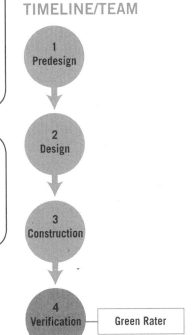

NOTES

- A project receiving points for EQ 1 is not eligible to earn points for EQ 4.3, but may earn points for EQ 4.2. A project pursuing EQ 4.3 must meet all the prerequisites in EQ 2–10.

- When the HVAC and heating and cooling system is being designed (EA 5, 6: EQ 4, 6) EQ 10.1 must be taken into consideration.

PRIMARY BENEFITS

- Improves indoor air quality.

- Improves durability of building components in the home (especially in the bathroom and kitchen areas).

STANDARDS

Section 5 of ASHRAE Standard 62.2-2007

Section 7 of ASHRAE Standard 62.2-2007

INTENT

Reduce moisture and exposure to indoor pollutants in kitchens and bathrooms.

REQUIREMENTS

- Bath and kitchen fans:

  ○ Design and install local exhausts in all bathrooms (including half-baths). Sample requirements that relate to minimum intermittent local exhaust flow rates are shown in the Table 1 on page 299 of the LEED for Homes Reference Guide, 2008.

  ○ Design and install a local exhaust in the kitchen.

  ○ Meet the requirements of Section 5 of ASHRAE Standard 62.2-2007.

- Design and install the fans and ducts to meet the requirements of Section 7 of ASHRAE Standard 62.2-2007.

- Exhaust air to the outdoors.

- Bathroom exhaust fans must be ENERGY STAR–labeled unless the bathroom is exhausted by a heat- or energy-recovery ventilator or the exhaust fan serves multiple bathrooms.

IMPLEMENTATION

- Many bath and kitchen exhaust systems are installed by the electrician, who does not typically understand air exhaust fundamentals. Either train the electrician in how to install the exhaust fans or have the HVAC contractor install them.

- If the fan ducting is long, ensure that the exhaust fan has the capacity to exhaust the amount of air needed.

VERIFICATION & SUBMITTALS

TRADE

- Provide calculations to the builder or project team leader demonstrating that the local exhaust system is designed to meet the requirements.

- Sign an Accountability Form to indicate that the local exhaust system is installed according to the design specifications.

- Provide any equipment literature (such as user manuals, brochures and specifications) to the builder or project team leader.

PROJECT TEAM

- Present calculations to the Green Rater demonstrating that the local exhaust system is designed to meet the requirements.

- Include any equipment literature in the occupant's operations and maintenance manual.

GREEN RATER

- Visually verify that all calculations for local exhaust are completed.

- Verify that an Accountability Form has been signed by the responsible party.

- Visually verify all applicable equipment in the home.

TIMELINE/TEAM

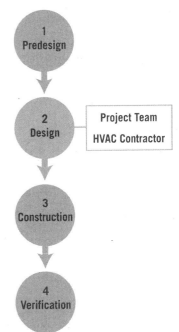

1 Predesign

2 Design — Project Team / HVAC Contractor

3 Construction

4 Verification

NOTES

- Exhausting air to attics or interstitial spaces is not permitted.

DOCUMENTATION & CALCULATIONS

- For kitchen fan air changes per hour:

  - ACH kitchen = Fan Capacity X 60 Minutes / Kitchen Size where ACH is the air changes per hour, fan capacity is measured in cfm, and kitchen size is measured in cubic feet.

  - If ACH kitchen is less than five, install the kitchen fan as a vented range hood.

PRIMARY BENEFITS

- Exhausts stale, moist air out of the home.

STANDARDS

None

INTENT

Reduce moisture and exposure to indoor pollutants in kitchens and bathrooms.

REQUIREMENTS

- Use one of the following strategies in every bathroom:

  - Occupancy sensor;
  - Automatic humidistat controller;
  - Automatic timer; or
  - Continuously operating exhaust fan.

- All fans in bathrooms, showers, bathtub areas or spas must meet the requirement for the point to be awarded.

IMPLEMENTATION

- A bathroom exhaust system is key to a good ventilation strategy for the home.

- An automatic switch that controls the length of time the exhaust fan operates can help reduce the moisture load in the bathroom.

- If the project is using an HRV or ERV, the system needs to have a higher setting for exhaust flow that is triggered when the bathrooms are used.

VERIFICATION & SUBMITTALS

TRADE

- Provide any equipment literature (such as user manuals, brochures and specifications) to the builder or project team leader.

PROJECT TEAM

- Include equipment literature on occupancy sensors, automatic humidistat controllers, automatic timers or continuously operating exhaust fans in the occupant's operations and maintenance manual.

GREEN RATER

- Visually verify applicable equipment in the home.

DOCUMENTATION & CALCULATIONS

None

TIMELINE/TEAM

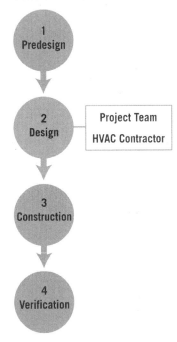

1 Predesign

2 Design — Project Team / HVAC Contractor

3 Construction

4 Verification

NOTES

- A project receiving points for EQ 1 is eligible to earn points for EQ 5.2 and EQ 5.3.

1 Point

PRIMARY BENEFITS

- Performance testing of the bath and kitchen fans ensures that they are operating as designed.

STANDARDS

ASHRAE 62.2-2007

INTENT

Reduce moisture and exposure to indoor pollutants in kitchens and bathrooms.

REQUIREMENTS

- Perform a third-party test of each exhaust airflow rate for compliance with Section 5 of ASHRAE Standard 62.2-2007.

IMPLEMENTATION

- If the performance test identifies a problem, the builder needs to bring the system into compliance for the point to be awarded.

VERIFICATION & SUBMITTALS

GREEN RATER

- Test exhaust airflow from the home and verify that it meets the requirements.

DOCUMENTATION & CALCULATIONS

- For kitchen fan air changes per hour:

  - ACH kitchen = Fan Capacity X 60 Minutes / Kitchen Size where ACH is the air changes per hour, fan capacity is measured in cfm, and kitchen size is measured in cubic feet.

  - If ACH kitchen is less than five, install the kitchen fan as a vented range hood.

TIMELINE/TEAM

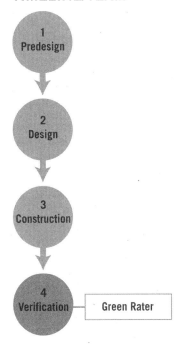

NOTES

- A project receiving points for EQ 1 is eligible to earn points for EQ 5.2 and EQ 5.3.

- Engage the third-party tester to perform the tests on the systems as soon as they can be tested to ensure that any problems that may surface can be addressed.

Required | **EQ 6: Distribution of Space Heating and Cooling**
EQ Prerequisite 6.1: Room-by-Room Load Calculations

PRIMARY BENEFITS

- Improves comfort.

- Improves moisture control.

INTENT

Provide appropriate distribution of space heating and cooling in the home to improve thermal comfort and energy performance.

STANDARDS

ACCA Manuals J and D

REQUIREMENTS

- There are two pathways for this measure, forced-air systems and nonducted systems.

  - Forced-air systems:
    - Perform design calculations and install ducts accordingly.
    - Use ACCA Manuals J and D, the ASHRAE Handbook of Fundamentals, or an equivalent computation procedure.

  - Nonducted HVAC systems (such as hydronic systems):
    - Perform the design calculations and the system accordingly.
    - Use ACCA Manuals J and D, the ASHRAE Handbook of Fundamentals, or an equivalent computation procedure.

IMPLEMENTATION

- Design the ducting system using ACCA Manuals J and D.

- The choice of air filter should be made prior to duct design, to ensure adequate air flow.

VERIFICATION & SUBMITTALS

TRADE

- Provide system design calculations to the project team.

- Sign an Accountability Form.

PROJECT TEAM

- Present design calculations to the Green Rater.

- Include any equipment literature in the occupant's operations and maintenance manual.

GREEN RATER

- Visually verify that all design calculations are completed.

- Verify that equipment has been installed.

- Verify that an Accountability Form has been signed.

DOCUMENTATION & CALCULATIONS

- No calculations need to be performed by the project team. These calculations are performed by a HVAC contractor or a mechanical engineer. Full Manuals J and D calculations are strongly recommended, but other software programs are available to assist HVAC contractors and mechanical engineers.

TIMELINE/TEAM

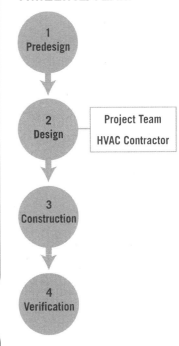

1 Predesign

2 Design — Project Team / HVAC Contractor

3 Construction

4 Verification

NOTES

- Proper sizing of the ducting is important to deliver the designed airflows to the rooms of the home. If the ducts are undersized or oversized, the room will become uncomfortable because too little or too much conditioned air is delivered.

- Under/oversized equipment can also cause performance issues which lead to efficiency losses and equipment failure.

EQ Credit 6.2: Forced-Air Systems—Return-Air Flow or Room-by-Room Controls (1 point)

EQ Credit 6.2: Nonducted HVAC Systems—Room-by-Room Controls (1 point)

PRIMARY BENEFITS

- Ensures proper distribution of heating and cooling.

STANDARDS

ACCA Manuals J and D

INTENT

Provide appropriate distribution of space heating and cooling in the home to improve thermal comfort and energy performance.

REQUIREMENTS

- There are two pathways for this measure, forced-air systems and nonducted systems.

  - Forced-air systems—return-air flow or room-by-room controls:

    - Ensure that every room (except baths, kitchens, closets, pantries and laundry rooms) has adequate return-air flow through the use of multiple returns, transfer grilles or jump ducts. Meet one of the following:

      - Size the opening to 1 square inch per cfm of supply, or

      - Demonstrate that the pressure differential between closed rooms and adjacent spaces with returns is no greater than 2.5 Pa.

  - Nonducted HVAC systems (such as hydronic systems)—room-by-room controls:

    - Design the HVAC system with flow-control valves on every radiator.

IMPLEMENTATION

- Using Manuals J and D, size the equipment and ducting or hydronic systems to provide proper delivery of conditioned air.

- For forced-air systems: Providing return-air flow pathways helps ensure that the air distribution system will work as designed.

IMPLEMENTATION, CONTINUED

- For nonducted systems: Providing room-by-room controls allows for fine-tuning the system to provide proper heating to separate areas.

- The choice of air filter should be made prior to duct design, to ensure adequate air flow.

VERIFICATION & SUBMITTALS

TRADE

- For ducted systems, provide calculations.

PROJECT TEAM

- For ducted systems, provide calculations to the Green Rater.

GREEN RATER

- For ducted systems, visually verify that all necessary calculations are completed.

- For nonducted systems, visually verify that each room has a flow-control valve.

DOCUMENTATION & CALCULATIONS

- Full ACCA Manuals J and D calculations are strongly recommended, but other software programs are available to assist HVAC contractors and mechanical engineers.

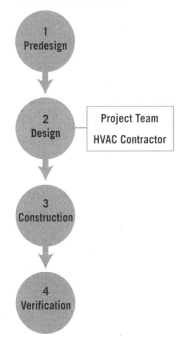

TIMELINE/TEAM

1 Predesign

2 Design — Project Team / HVAC Contractor

3 Construction

4 Verification

NOTES

- A project receiving points for EQ 1 is not eligible to earn points for EQ 6.2 or EQ 6.3. A project pursuing EQ 6.2 or EQ 6.3 must meet all the prerequisites in EQ 2–10.

- When the HVAC and heating and cooling system is being designed (EA 5, 6; EQ 4, 6) EQ 10.1 must be taken into consideration.

EQ Credit 6.3: Forced-Air Systems—Third-Party Performance Test
(2 points)

EQ Credit 6.3: Nonducted HVAC Systems—Multiple Zones
(2 points)

PRIMARY BENEFITS

- Third-party performance testing helps determine that the air distribution system is working as designed.

STANDARDS

ACCA Manuals J and D

INTENT

Provide appropriate distribution of space heating and cooling in the home to improve thermal comfort and energy performance.

REQUIREMENTS

- There are two pathways for this measure, forced-air systems and nonducted systems.
  - Forced-air systems—third-party performance test:
    - Have the total supply-air flow rates in each room tested using a flow hood with doors closed or other approved methods. Meet the following:
      - Supply-air flow rates must be within +/- 15% (or +/- 10 cfm) of calculated values from ACCA Manual J (as required by EA 6.1).
  - Nonducted HVAC systems (such as hydronic systems)—multiple zones:
    - Install nonducted HVAC system:
      - Minimum of two distinct zones.
      - With independent thermostat controls.
      - These controls must be occupant-controlled.

IMPLEMENTATION

- Engage the third-party tester to perform the tests on the systems as soon as they can be tested to see whether there are any problems that might need to be addressed.

- The choice of air filter should be made prior to duct design, to ensure adequate air flow.

VERIFICATION & SUBMITTALS

GREEN RATER

- For ducted systems, conduct testing of supply-air flow rates in each room and verify that the requirements are met.

- For nonducted systems, visually verify zones and thermostat controls.

DOCUMENTATION & CALCULATIONS

- Complete Manuals J and D calculations are strongly recommended, but other software programs are available to assist HVAC contractors and mechanical engineers.

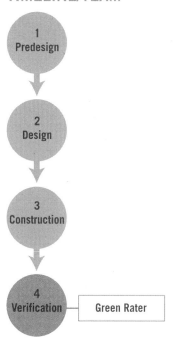

TIMELINE/TEAM

1 Predesign

2 Design

3 Construction

4 Verification — Green Rater

NOTES

- A project receiving points for EQ 1 is not eligible to earn points for EQ 6.2 or EQ 6.3. A project pursuing EQ 6.2 or EQ 6.3 must meet all the prerequisites in EQ 2–10.

- When the HVAC and heating and cooling system is being designed (EA 5, 6: EQ 4, 6) EQ 10.1 must be taken into consideration.

PRIMARY BENEFITS

- Filtration of indoor and incoming air improves the air quality.

STANDARDS

ASHRAE Standard 52.2 for MERV ratings

INTENT

Reduce particulate matter from the air supply system.

REQUIREMENTS

- There are two pathways for this measure, forced-air systems and nonducted systems.

  ○ Forced-air systems:
    - Install air filters with a minimum efficiency reporting value (MERV) ≥ 8 and ensure that the air handler can maintain adequate pressure and airflow.
    - Mini-split systems and PTAC units are exempt from meeting the MERV requirements for this measure.
    - Projects with a mechanical supply system that is separate from the air handler unit that draws outdoor air into the home must meet the requirements of a MERV 8 or better filter in the system to qualify.

  ○ Nonducted HVAC systems (such as hydronic systems):
    - Install air filters with a MERV ≥ 8 and ensure that the air handler can maintain adequate pressure and airflow.
    - A home in a climate with fewer than 4,500 infiltration degree-days is exempt from this requirement.
    - A home that uses only passive or exhaust-only ventilation is exempt from this requirement.

IMPLEMENTATION

- Investigate the opportunity for using better filters. Select the air filter before the ducts have been sized to ensure that adequate airflow can be achieved.

- True HEPA filters meet MERV 16.

- Electronic filters cannot be rated using the MERV protocol and, therefore, do not qualify as an appropriate filtration strategy.

IMPLEMENTATION, CONTINUED

- High-efficiency air filters can restrict airflow in the ducting system; therefore, the HVAC contractor needs to ensure that the system is appropriately sized.

- The choice of air filter should be made prior to duct design, to ensure adequate air flow.

TIMELINE/TEAM

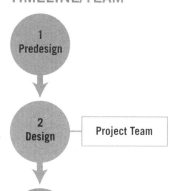

VERIFICATION & SUBMITTALS

TRADE

- Provide any air filter literature to the builder or project team leader.

PROJECT TEAM

- Present any air filter literature to the Green Rater.

- Include product literature in the occupant's operations and maintenance manual.

GREEN RATER

- Visually verify that the applicable MERV rating has been met.

- Visually verify air filters and housing in the home.

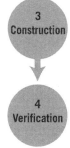

NOTES

None

DOCUMENTATION & CALCULATIONS

None

PRIMARY BENEFITS

- Reduces particulate matter.

STANDARDS

ASHRAE Standard 52.2 for MERV ratings

INTENT

Reduce particulate matter from the air supply system.

REQUIREMENTS

- There are two pathways for this measure; ducted systems and nonducted systems.

  - Ducted systems:
    - EQ 7.2: Better Filters—Install air filters with a minimum efficiency reporting value (MERV) ≥ 10 and ensure that the air handler can maintain adequate pressure and airflow (1 point).
    - EQ 7.3: Best Filters—Install air filters with a MERV ≥ 13 and ensure that the air handler can maintain adequate pressure and airflow (2 points).

  - Nonducted systems:
    - EQ 7.2: Better Filters—Install air filters with a MERV ≥ 10 and ensure that the air handler can maintain adequate pressure and airflow (1 point).
    - EQ 7.3: Best Filters—Install air filters with a MERV ≥ 13 and ensure that the air handler can maintain adequate pressure and airflow (2 points).

IMPLEMENTATION

- Investigate the opportunity for using better filters. Select the air filter before the ducts have been sized to ensure adequate airflow.

VERIFICATION & SUBMITTALS

TRADE

- Provide any air filter literature to the builder or project team leader.

PROJECT TEAM

- Present any air filter literature to the Green Rater.

- Include product literature in the occupant's operations and maintenance manual.

GREEN RATER

- Visually verify that the applicable MERV rating has been met.

- Visually verify air filters and housing in the home.

DOCUMENTATION & CALCULATIONS

None

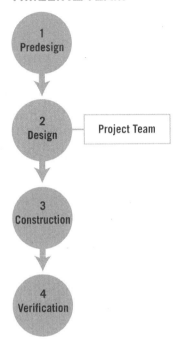

TIMELINE/TEAM

1 Predesign

2 Design — Project Team

3 Construction

4 Verification

NOTES

- A project receiving points for EQ 1 is eligible to earn points for EQ 7.2 or EQ 7.3.

- True HEPA filters meet MERV 16.

- Electronic filters cannot be rated using the MERV protocol and, therefore, do not qualify as an appropriate filtration strategy.

- High-efficiency air filters can restrict airflow in the ducting system; therefore, the HVAC contractor needs to ensure that the system is appropriately sized.

- The choice of air filter should be made prior to duct design, to ensure adequate air flow.

1 Point | **EQ 8: Contaminant Control, EQ Credit 8.1: Indoor Contaminant Control During Construction**

PRIMARY BENEFITS

- Improves indoor air quality.

- Protects the heat exchanger in the furnace and duct termination points from particulate matter once they have been installed thus reducing the chance that the ducts will distribute particulate matter throughout the home once the system is operational.

STANDARDS

None

INTENT

Reduce occupants' and construction workers' exposure to indoor airborne contaminants through source control and removal.

REQUIREMENTS

- Upon installation, seal all permanent ducts and vents to minimize contamination during construction. Remove any seals after all phases of construction are completed.

- This credit is not awarded automatically to projects with nonducted systems. Projects with nonducted systems must submit a CIR to earn the point. Within the CIR, the project must demonstrate an effort to reduce occupants' exposure to construction pollutants.

IMPLEMENTATION

- Seal the ducts once they have been installed. This can be accomplished by screwing a cover over the duct hole in the floor or using a predesigned cover.

VERIFICATION & SUBMITTALS

PROJECT TEAM

- Sign an Accountability Form to indicate that the system is installed according to the design specifications.

GREEN RATER

- During construction, visually verify that ducts are sealed at the termination point.

- After construction, conduct a visual inspection and swipe of duct interiors.

- Verify that an Accountability Form has been signed by the responsible party.

DOCUMENTATION & CALCULATIONS

None

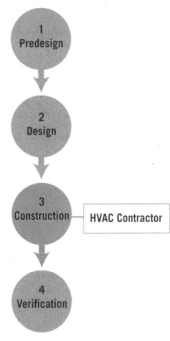

TIMELINE/TEAM

1 Predesign

2 Design

3 Construction — HVAC Contractor

4 Verification

NOTES

- A project receiving points for EQ 1 is not eligible to earn points for EQ 8.1 or EQ 8.3, but may earn points for EQ 8.2. A project pursuing EQ 8.2 must meet all the prerequisites in EQ 2–10.

PRIMARY BENEFITS

- Reducing particulate matter improves indoor air quality.

STANDARDS

None

INTENT

Reduce occupants' and construction workers' exposure to indoor airborne contaminants through source control and removal.

REQUIREMENTS

- Select from the following measures (one point each, for a total of two points awarded):

  ○ Design and install a permanent walk-off mat at each entry that is at least 4 feet in length and allow for cleaning.

  ○ Design a shoe removal and storage space near the primary entryway. It must hold two pairs of shoes for each bedroom of the home. This space may not have wall-to-wall carpeting.

  ○ Install a central vacuum system with exhaust to the exterior.

Exemplary Performance: Projects that implement all three strategies can earn one additional point under ID 3.

IMPLEMENTATION

- All three strategies are designed to reduce particulate matter in the home at different stages. A comprehensive strategy will address a number of these strategies.

VERIFICATION & SUBMITTALS

PROJECT TEAM

- Include any central vacuum system equipment literature in the occupant's operations and maintenance manual.

GREEN RATER

- Visually verify walk-off mats, shoe storage areas, and/or a central vacuum system in the home.

DOCUMENTATION & CALCULATIONS

None

TIMELINE/TEAM

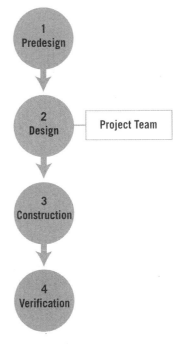

NOTES

- A project receiving points for EQ 1 is not eligible to earn points for EQ 8.1 or EQ 8.3, but may earn points for EQ 8.2. A project pursuing EQ 8.2 must meet all the prerequisites in EQ 2–10.

PRIMARY BENEFITS

- Reducing indoor air contaminants at the end of construction can improve the indoor air quality of the home prior to move-in.

STANDARDS

None

INTENT

Reduce occupants' and construction workers' exposure to indoor airborne contaminants through source control and removal.

REQUIREMENTS

- Flush the home with fresh air, according to the following guidelines:
  - Flush prior to occupancy, but after all phases of construction are complete.
  - Flush the entire home, keeping all interior doors open.
  - Flush for 48 hours total; the hours may be nonconsecutive.
  - Keep all windows open and run a fan continuously, or flush the home with all HVAC fans and exhaust fans operating continuously at the highest flow rate.
  - Use additional fans to circulate air within the home.
  - Replace or clean HVAC air filters afterward, as necessary.

IMPLEMENTATION

- Determine the best time to implement this measure. If the homeowner is ready to move in at the end of construction, meet with the homeowner to explain the benefits of this measure to allow enough time for the preoccupancy flush to take place.

VERIFICATION & SUBMITTALS

PROJECT TEAM

- Sign an Accountability Form to indicate that the preoccupancy flush has been conducted according to the requirements.

GREEN RATER

- Verify that an Accountability Form has been signed by the responsible party.

DOCUMENTATION & CALCULATIONS

None

TIMELINE/TEAM

1 Predesign

2 Design

3 Construction — Project Team

4 Verification

NOTES

- A project receiving points for EQ 1 is not eligible to earn points for EQ 8.1 or EQ 8.3, but may earn points for EQ 8.2. A project pursuing EQ 8.2 must meet all the prerequisites in EQ 2–10.

EQ Prerequisite 9.1: Radon-Resistant Construction in High-Risk Areas (Required)

EQ Credit 9.2: Radon-Resistant Construction in Moderate-Risk Areas (1 point)

PRIMARY BENEFITS

- Reducing the opportunity for radon to enter the home reduces the potential health hazard radon gas poses.

STANDARDS

The EPA's "Building Radon Out: A Step-by-Step Guide on How to Build Radon-Resistant Homes."

International Residential Code, Appendix F

Washington State Ventilation and Indoor Air Quality Code

INTENT

Reduce occupant exposure to radon gas and other soil gas contaminants.

REQUIREMENTS

Requirements EQ 9.1:

- If the home is in Environmental Protection Agency Radon Zone 1, design and build the home with radon-resistant construction techniques.

- The requirements for radon protection are automatically satisfied if the home is elevated by at least 2 feet, with open air space between the home and ground. An open-air garage under a multifamily building is an acceptable alternative.

Requirements EQ 9.2:

- If a home is in Environmental Protection Agency Radon Zone 2 or 3, design and build the home with radon-resistant construction techniques.

- The requirements for radon protection are automatically satisfied if the home is elevated by at least 2 feet, with open air space between the home and ground. An open-air garage under a multifamily building is an acceptable alternative.

IMPLEMENTATION

- Investigate the EPA's radon-resistant construction techniques and implement applicable measures on the project.

- Radon-resistant construction strategies comprise the following components: a gas-permeable layer, heavy-gauge plastic sheeting, the sealing and caulking of all penetrations through the concrete slab, and a vent pipe to exhaust gases from under the home to the exterior of the home.

IMPLEMENTATION, CONTINUED

- Gut-rehab projects should use the new residential construction guidance in Indoor airPLUS, or the existing residential buildings language in ASTM Standard E2121. Post-occupancy tests are strongly encouraged.

VERIFICATION & SUBMITTALS

PROJECT TEAM

- Sign an Accountability Form to indicate that the home was built with radon-resistant construction.

GREEN RATER

- Visually verify radon-resistant construction.

- Verify that an Accountability Form has been signed by the responsible party.

DOCUMENTATION & CALCULATIONS

None

TIMELINE/TEAM

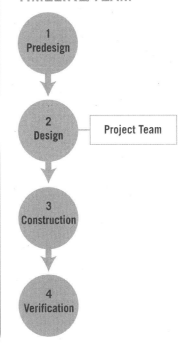

1 Predesign

2 Design — Project Team

3 Construction

4 Verification

NOTES

- Radon-resistant construction does not guarantee that occupants will not be exposed to radon. The Surgeon General and the EPA recommend that every home in the country be tested for radon. Information about radon testing is available at the EPA website, at http://www.epa.gov/radon/proficiency.html.

PRIMARY BENEFITS

- Keeping the HVAC system out of the garage reduces the opportunity for gases from the garage to enter the home.

STANDARDS

None

INTENT

Reduce occupant exposure to indoor pollutants originating from an adjacent garage.

REQUIREMENTS

- Place all air-handling equipment and ductwork outside the fire-rated envelope of the garage.

IMPLEMENTATION

- Examine options outside the garage where the HVAC system can be placed. If the HVAC system needs to be in the garage, build a mechanical room that is air-sealed from the garage and has its own air supply.

VERIFICATION & SUBMITTALS

GREEN RATER

- Visually verify that all prerequisite requirements are met.

DOCUMENTATION & CALCULATIONS

None

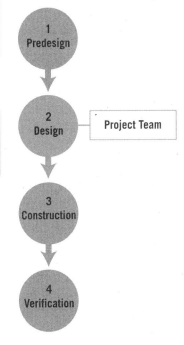

TIMELINE/TEAM

1 Predesign

2 Design — Project Team

3 Construction

4 Verification

NOTES

- When the HVAC and heating and cooling system is being designed (EA 5, 6; EQ 4, 6) EQ 10.1 must be taken into consideration.

2 Points | **EQ 10: Garage Pollutant Protection**
EQ Credit 10.2: Minimize Pollutants From Garage

PRIMARY BENEFITS

- Sealing the garage from the home reduces the opportunity for garage pollutants to enter the home. The garage typically harbors a number of pollutants, such as lawnmower and automobile fumes, fertilizers, pesticides, herbicides, paint and solvents, among other items.

STANDARDS

None

INTENT

Reduce occupant exposure to indoor pollutants originating from an adjacent garage.

REQUIREMENTS

- Tightly seal shared surfaces between the garage and conditioned spaces, including all of the following:

  ○ In conditioned spaces above garages:
    - Seal all penetrations.
    - Seal all connecting floor and ceiling joist bays.
    - Paint walls and ceilings.

  ○ In conditioned spaces next to the garage:
    - Weather-strip all doors.
    - Place carbon monoxide (CO_2) detectors in adjacent rooms that share a door with the garage.
    - Seal all penetrations.
    - Seal all cracks at the base of the walls.

IMPLEMENTATION

- The garage is typically built as part of the home, thus, the wall between the garage and the living space provides many pathways for pollutants to enter the living space. Care must be taken in creating an airtight barrier between the garage and living space.

VERIFICATION & SUBMITTALS

GREEN RATER

- Visually verify that the requirements have been met.

DOCUMENTATION & CALCULATIONS

None

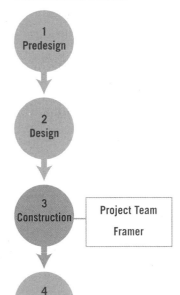

TIMELINE/TEAM

1 Predesign

2 Design

3 Construction — Project Team / Framer

4 Verification

NOTES

- A project receiving points for EQ 1 is not eligible to earn points for EQ 10.2, EQ 10.3, or EQ 10.4. A project receiving points EQ 10.4 is not eligible to earn points for EQ 10.2 or 10.3, and vice versa.

PRIMARY BENEFITS

- The garage is a place where many pollutants can accumulate, especially automobile exhaust. Installing an exhaust fan in the garage that operates automatically to exhaust pollutants thus reduces the opportunity for the pollutants to enter the home.

STANDARDS

None

INTENT

Reduce occupant exposure to indoor pollutants originating from an adjacent garage.

REQUIREMENTS

- Install an exhaust fan in the garage that is rated for continuous use and designed to operate in one of the following ways:

  ○ Nonducted fan must be 70 cfm (or greater) or a ducted fan must be 100 cfm or greater;

  ○ Fan must run continuously; or

  ○ Fan must be designed with an automatic controller.
    - The fan must provide at least three air changes each time it is turned on.

IMPLEMENTATION

- Investigate locations for placement of the exhaust fan and which automatic controller will work best for the home being built.

VERIFICATION & SUBMITTALS

TRADE

- Provide calculations to the builder or project team leader demonstrating that the garage exhaust fan provides the necessary air changes.

- Deliver any garage exhaust fan equipment literature to the builder or project team leader.

PROJECT TEAM

- Provide calculations to the Green Rater demonstrating that the garage exhaust fan provides the necessary air changes.

- Include garage exhaust fan equipment literature in the occupant's operations and maintenance manual.

GREEN RATER

- Visually verify the calculations for garage air changes.

- Visually verify that the appropriate garage exhaust equipment has been installed.

TIMELINE/TEAM

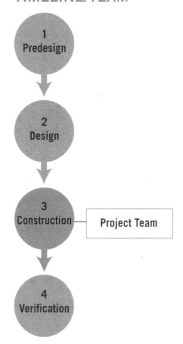

1 Predesign

2 Design

3 Construction — Project Team

4 Verification

NOTES

- A project receiving points for EQ 1 is not eligible to earn points for EQ 10.2, EQ 10.3, or EQ 10.4. A project receiving points EQ 10.4 is not eligible to earn points for EQ 10.2 or 10.3, and vice versa.

DOCUMENTATION & CALCULATIONS

- Calculations must be performed to determine how long the exhaust fan must operate.

- Operating Time = (Garage Size X 3) / Fan Capacity

- Garage Size = Height X Width X Length

  Sample calculation:

  A 20-by-15-by-9-foot garage has 2,700 cubic feet. Three air changes cover 8,100 cubic feet. A 100-cfm fan must be set to run for 81 minutes.

3 Points | **EQ 10: Garage Pollutant Protection**
EQ Credit 10.4: Detached Garage or No Garage

PRIMARY BENEFITS

- Designing a home with a detached garage or no garage is the best strategy to reduce the opportunity for garage pollutants to enter the home.

- Reduces material use when no garage is built.

STANDARDS

None

INTENT

Reduce occupant exposure to indoor pollutants originating from an adjacent garage.

REQUIREMENTS

- The home has a detached garage or has no garage.

IMPLEMENTATION

- Design the home with no garage.

- Design the home with a detached garage.

- If the home has a detached garage, more land is typically needed to accommodate that strategy.

VERIFICATION & SUBMITTALS

GREEN RATER

- Visually verify that the home has no attached garage.

DOCUMENTATION & CALCULATIONS

None

TIMELINE/TEAM

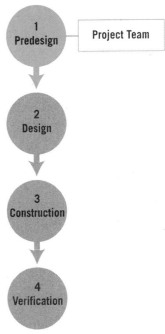

1 Predesign — Project Team

2 Design

3 Construction

4 Verification

NOTES

- A project receiving points for EQ 1 is not eligible to earn points for EQ 10.2, EQ 10.3, or EQ 10.4. A project receiving points EQ 10.4 is not eligible to earn points for EQ 10.2 or 10.3, and vice versa.

EQ CATEGORY REVIEW

1 Which credits fall within the performance pathway in the Indoor Environmental Quality category?

_____

_____

2 What is the referenced standard in Indoor Environmental Quality for ventilation and exhaust?

_____

_____

3 What are some of the components of radon-resistant construction?

_____

_____

4 What should the HVAC contractor take into account when sizing equipment, ducts, and grilles?

_____

_____

EQ LEARNING ACTIVITIES

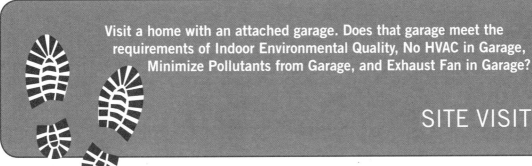

Visit a home with an attached garage. Does that garage meet the requirements of Indoor Environmental Quality, No HVAC in Garage, Minimize Pollutants from Garage, and Exhaust Fan in Garage?

SITE VISIT

Determine the MERV ratings of air filters in the HVAC system in your home.

INVESTIGATE

Visit the EPA Indoor airPLUS website, www.epa.gov/indoorairplus. Read about the features and advantages of Indoor airPLUS.

FIND OUT MORE

1 A bathroom fan rated at 80 cfm has been installed and meets the prerequisite airflow rate. When the performance test was conducted, the test resulted in a performance of 40 cfm. What do they need to do to earn the point for the third-party performance testing?

A) They don't have to do anything because it already qualifies.

B) They need to conduct a second performance test to meet section 5 of ASHRAE 62.2-2007.

C) They need to increase the air flow rate and conduct a second performance test.

D) They need to decrease the air flow rate and conduct a second performance test.

2 According to Indoor Environmental Quality 8, Contaminant Control, a preoccupancy flush with windows open requires what length of time and method?

A) 24 hours, all HVAC fans run at maximum air flow plus additional internal fans running.

B) 48 hours, all HVAC fans run at maximum air flow plus additional internal fans running.

C) 72 hours, all HVAC fans run at minimum air flow.

D) 72 hours, all HVAC fans run at minimum air flow plus additional internal fans running.

See Answer Key on page 270.

3 How many CO_2 monitors should be installed in a 2-story home that is built over a basement and has an attached garage that is heated by a heat pump and does not have any combustion sources installed in the house?

A) One for each floor of the house.

B) One in the room that is adjacent to the garage.

C) None, there are no combustion sources in the house.

D) One for each floor of the house and potentially one in the room that is adjacent to the garage.

4 You have decided that a MERV 13 filter will be installed on the furnace. To ensure that the mechanical system maintains adequate air flow, what does the project team need to do?

A) Design the system with the filter rating in mind.

B) Incorporate a heat recovery ventilator into the mechanical system.

C) Install a furnace that is at least 90% energy efficient.

D) Increase the size of the furnace.

5 How do the MERV ratings for electronic filters compare to the MERV ratings for non-electronic filters?

A) Electronic filters have much higher ratings.

B) Electronic filters have much lower ratings.

C) Electronic filters cannot be MERV rated.

D) Electronic filters are more efficient.

AWARENESS & EDUCATION

The Awareness & Education (AE) category promotes broad awareness among home buyers and tenants that **LEED**-certified homes are built differently and need to be operated and maintained accordingly.

WHAT ABOUT AWARENESS & EDUCATION?

What happens to an efficient light fixture if it is improperly used?

How long should a new home last?

How much energy, water and other resources will be consumed over the lifetime of a home?

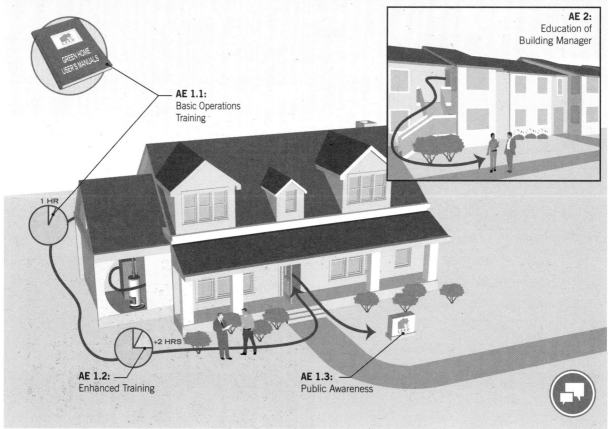

AE 2:
Education of
Building Manager

AE 1.1:
Basic Operations
Training

1 HR

+2 HRS

AE 1.2:
Enhanced Training

AE 1.3:
Public Awareness

GREEN HOME
USER'S MANUALS

THE OVERVIEW

The environmental impact of a home continues throughout its life cycle, well beyond the initial design and construction decisions. Occupants play a substantial role in the resource use of a home over its lifetime.

Some home buyers may know very little about green home construction. They may be unaware of the green features in the home, or they may be unfamiliar with how to use and maintain them. Without adequate training, the full benefits of the LEED measures likely will not be achieved.

As noted above, the AE category promotes broad awareness among buyers and tenants about the differences in features and operations and maintenance between a conventional home and a LEED-certified home. In addition, because the operations and maintenance tasks in multifamily buildings may be performed by a building manager, this credit addresses the need for appropriate education of building managers, as well.

AWARENESS & EDUCATION

SYNERGIES

The prerequisites and credits in this category help pull the whole process of building a high performance home together. They do this by helping provide educational tools for homebuyers. By providing educational resources and training to the home buyer, rental tenants and the public, the homebuilder is able to pass on the knowledge on how to keep the high performance features of the home operating the way they should for years to come.

THE CREDITS

AE		
AE 1: Education of the Homeowner/ Tenant	This credit requires the project team to provide an occupant's manual and conduct a walk-through with the home buyer. It rewards those who further educate their home buyers, rental tenants and the public.
AE 2: Education of the Building Manager	This credit rewards the project team that educates building managers and provides them with a building manager's manual.

KEY TERMS

Homeowner Manual	An operations and maintenance manual or binder that includes all the following items: The completed LEED checklist, accountability forms and durability inspection checklist. Product manuals on all installed equipment, fixtures and appliances as well as operations and maintenance guidance for any LEED related equipment. General educational information on green power, efficient use of energy and resources as well as occupant activities and choices (such as cleaning products and lighting selection).

PRIMARY BENEFITS

- Provides the homeowner with information about maintaining and operating the home.

STANDARDS

None

INTENT

Maintain the performance of the home by educating the occupants (the homeowners or tenants) about the operations and maintenance of the home's LEED features and equipment.

REQUIREMENTS

- Develop and provide the home's occupant with an operations and maintenance manual including the following:
  - Completed LEED for Homes Checklist;
  - Copy of each signed Accountability Form;
  - Copy of the durability inspection checklist;
  - Product manufacturers' manuals for all installed equipment;
  - General information on efficient use of energy, water and natural resources;
  - Educational information on "green power";
  - Operations and maintenance guidance for any LEED for Homes-related equipment in the home:
    - Space heating equipment;
    - Mechanical ventilation equipment;
    - Humidity control equipment;
    - Radon protection system;
    - Renewable energy system; and
    - Irrigation, rainwater harvesting and graywater systems.
  - Guidance on occupant activities and choices, including:
    - Cleaning materials, methods and supplies;
    - Water-efficient landscaping;
    - Impact of chemical fertilizers and pesticides;
    - Irrigation;
    - Lighting selection; and
    - Appliance selection.
- A minimum one-hour walk-through of the home with the occupant(s), featuring the following:
  - Identification of all installed items;
  - Instructions on how to apply the measures and operate the equipment; and
  - Information on how to maintain the measures and equipment.

IMPLEMENTATION

- Start developing and/or collecting the required items for inclusion in the operations and maintenance manual as soon as possible.

- There are several sample homeowner manuals builders can purchase and modify for their particular use.

VERIFICATION & SUBMITTALS

PROJECT TEAM

- Present the operations and maintenance manual to the Green Rater for review.

- Provide the operations and maintenance manual to the occupant.

- Sign the Accountability Form to indicate that a walk-through has been conducted with the occupant.

GREEN RATER

- Visually verify that the operations and maintenance manual meets the requirements.

- Verify that an Accountability Form has been signed by the responsible party.

DOCUMENTATION & CALCULATIONS

None

TIMELINE/TEAM

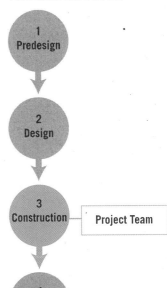

NOTES

- Many of the measures in the Rating System should be addressed in the operations manual and the on-site training.

1 Point | **AE 1: Education of the Homeowner or Tenant**
AE Credit 1.2: Enhanced Training

PRIMARY BENEFITS

- Provides the homeowner with information about maintaining and operating the home.

STANDARDS

None

INTENT

Maintain the performance of the home by educating the occupants (the homeowners or tenants) about the operations and maintenance of the home's LEED features and equipment.

REQUIREMENTS

- Provide two hours of training in addition to the training provided in AE 1.1.

IMPLEMENTATION

- Use a similar home to perform the additional walk-through.

- Use a builder- or developer-sponsored meeting of potential home buyers that informs participants of the unique features of the home.

- Conduct a group home buyer training.

- Develop a DVD with operations and maintenance information about the home's LEED for Homes measures.

- There are a number of sample homeowner manuals that builders can purchase and modify for their particular use.

VERIFICATION & SUBMITTALS

PROJECT TEAM

- Sign an Accountability Form to indicate that additional training that meets the requirements has been provided to the occupant.

GREEN RATER

- Verify that an Accountability Form has been signed by the responsible party.

DOCUMENTATION & CALCULATIONS

None

TIMELINE/TEAM

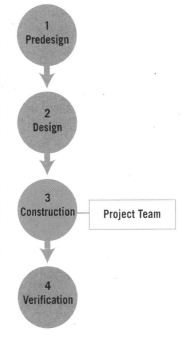

NOTES

- Many of the measures in the Rating System should be addressed in the operations manual and the on-site training.

1 Point

AE 1: Education of the Homeowner or Tenant
AE Credit 1.3: Public Awareness

PRIMARY BENEFITS

- Promoting public awareness of LEED for Homes and the project team's involvement in the program helps communicate the project has achieved a high standard of energy and environmental performance on the houses they have built.

STANDARDS

None

INTENT

Maintain the performance of the home by educating the occupants (the homeowners or tenants) about the operations and maintenance of the home's LEED features and equipment.

REQUIREMENTS

Promote general public awareness about LEED for Homes by conducting at least three of the following:

- Hold an advertised, attended open home that lasts at least four hours per day over four weekends with displays in the home that feature at least four informational stations about LEED for Homes features.

  OR

- Participate in a green building exhibition or tour with displays in the home that feature at least four informational stations about LEED for Homes features.

  AND/OR

- Publish a website with at least two pages that provide detailed information about the features and benefits of LEED for Homes.

- Generate a newspaper article about a LEED for Homes project.

- Display LEED for Homes signage, measuring 6 square feet or more, on the exterior of the home or building.

IMPLEMENTATION

- Develop a marketing/promotions plan if the home is a market-rate home.

VERIFICATION & SUBMITTALS

PROJECT TEAM

- Provide open-house dates, website addresses and/or newspaper citations to the Green Rater.

GREEN RATER

- Visually verify the list of open-house dates, website pages, newspaper articles and LEED for Homes signage.

DOCUMENTATION & CALCULATIONS

None

TIMELINE/TEAM

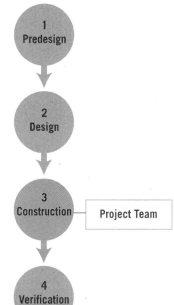

NOTES

None

PRIMARY BENEFITS

- Provides the maintenance staff with information about maintaining and operating the building.

STANDARDS

None

INTENT

Maintain the performance of the home by educating the building manager about the operations and maintenance of the home's LEED features and equipment.

REQUIREMENTS

This credit is available for multi-family projects only.

- Develop and provide the building manager with an operations and maintenance manual including the following:
  - Completed LEED for Homes Checklist;
  - Copy of each signed Accountability Form;
  - Copy of the durability inspection checklist;
  - Product manufacturers' manuals for all installed equipment;
  - General information on efficient use of energy, water and natural resources;
  - Educational information on "green power";
  - Operations and maintenance guidance for any LEED for Homes–related equipment in the home:
    - Space heating equipment;
    - Mechanical ventilation equipment;
    - Humidity control equipment;
    - Radon protection system;
    - Renewable energy system; and
    - Irrigation, rainwater harvesting and graywater systems.
  - Guidance on occupant activities and choices, including:
    - Cleaning materials, methods and supplies;
    - Water-efficient landscaping;
    - Impact of chemical fertilizers and pesticides;
    - Irrigation;
    - Lighting selection; and
    - Appliance selection.
- A minimum one-hour walk-through of the building before occupancy, featuring the following:
  - Identification of all installed items;
  - Instructions on how to apply the measures and operate the equipment in each unit; and
  - Information on how to maintain the measures and equipment in each unit.

| Exemplary Performance | No |

IMPLEMENTATION

- Start developing and/or collecting the required items for inclusion in the operations and maintenance manual as soon as possible.

VERIFICATION & SUBMITTALS

PROJECT TEAM

- Present the operations and maintenance manual to the Green Rater for review.

- Provide the operations and maintenance manual to the building manager.

- Sign the Accountability Form to indicate that a walk-through has been conducted with the building manager.

GREEN RATER

- Visually verify that the operations and maintenance manual meets the requirements.

- Verify that an Accountability Form has been signed by the responsible party.

TIMELINE/TEAM

1 Predesign

2 Design

3 Construction —— Project Team

4 Verification

NOTES

None

DOCUMENTATION & CALCULATIONS

None

1 What are some strategies for educating homeowners/tenants on maintaining the performance of their LEED-certified home?

_____

_____

2 What are some of the items that need to be included in the operations and maintenance manual given to the building manager to achieve AE 2?

_____

_____

3 What is the intent of AE 1, Education of the homeowner or tenant? What are the benefits associated with achieving this measure?

_____

_____

Request to shadow a traditional home inspector on their next home inspection. Then request to shadow a builder on their next walk-through with an occupant of a LEED certified home. How did the walk-throughs differ? How were they similar?

SITE VISIT

Ask around to discover the greatest challenges that homeowners and tenants experience when operating or maintaining green features in their home. Ask to see samples of homeowner/tenant manuals or educational materials.

ASK AROUND

1 The intent of the Awareness & Education Credit is to maintain the performance of the home by educating the occupants about the ____?

A) operations and maintenance of the home's LEED features and equipment.

B) costs associated with operating a LEED-certified home.

C) process and practices that were used in the LEED-certified home's design and construction.

D) energy efficiency savings the occupants can expect on their utility bills.

3 According to Awareness & Education measure 1.2: Enhanced Training, what are valid ways to conduct eligible enhanced training of occupants of homes?

A) An additional walk-through that takes one additional hour.

B) An additional walk-through that takes two additional hours.

C) A DVD that contains maintenance information about the home.

D) A group homebuyer training that covers the amenities of the project.

See Answer Key on page 270.

2 Under the Awareness & Education, Education of Building Manager credit, signing an Accountability Form indicates that the ____?

A) builder is no longer responsible for the building's operation and maintenance.

B) walk-through has been conducted with the building manager.

C) building manager has completed the paperwork to apply for LEED certification.

D) building manager agrees to stay in touch with the project team.

PRACTICE QUESTION ANSWER KEY

INNOVATION & DESIGN

1. **B.** Site issues need to be addressed early in the design phase or the opportunities are missed.

2. **D.** Innovative design requests should include the following information: intent, measures, proposed metric, verification and submittals, and proposed benefits.

3. **C.** Exemplary performance is earned by exceeding the requirements for a credit already awarded in the LEED for Homes Rating System. Exemplary performance credit is not available for every credit but is typically reserved for credits where exceeding the current requirements will yield a substantial environmental or human health benefit.

4. **D.** Interior moisture loads are considered a principal durability risk along with exterior water, air infiltration, interstitial condensation, heat loss, ultraviolet radiation, pest, and natural disasters.

LOCATION & LINKAGES

1. **A.** One point can be earned by selecting a lot that is within ½ mile of existing water service lines and sewer service lines.

2. **A.** One point can be earned for the Edge Development credit by selecting a lot such that at least 25% of the perimeter immediately borders previously developed land.

3. **C.** The best strategy for meeting the Site Selection credit is to build new homes on previously developed infill lots.

4. **C.** A site that meets the criteria of being located within ¼ mile of seven basic resources earns 2 points under credit 5.2 Extensive Community Resources / Feedback (p. 69).

5. **D.** Open spaces must consist predominantly of softscapes such as soil, grass, shrubs, and trees. These include natural open spaces; city, county, and state parks; play areas; and other community open spaces specifically intended for recreational use.

SUSTAINABLE SITES

1. **A, D.** In addition to causing soil erosion, construction can unnecessarily kill natural vegetation, including shrubs and trees, destroying habitat and displacing wildlife.

2. **C.** Invasive plant species that are not part of the landscape plan do not need to be removed from the site.

3. **C.** Reduction of the heat island effect minimizes disturbance of local microclimates and reduces summer cooling loads, which in turn reduce energy use, ground-level ozone, greenhouse gas and smog generation, and infrastructure requirements.

4. **B, D.** Design the lot such that at least 70% of the built environment, not including area under roof, is permeable or designed to capture water runoff for infiltration on-site. Area that can be counted toward the minimum includes vegetative landscape.

5. **C.** If a project reduces water demand by more than 45%, it is eligible to earn points in WE 2.3.

WATER EFFICIENCY

1. **D.** According to WE 1, Water Reuse, Table 1. Rainwater Harvesting, rainwater harvesting from 75% or more of the roof area for indoor and outdoor applications earns 4 points. Rainwater harvesting from 50% or more of the roof area for outdoor applications only earns 3 points, and rainwater harvesting from 50% or more of the roof area for indoor applications only earns 2 points.

2. **C.** Points earned under WE 2.1 High-Efficiency Irrigation System are for irrigation systems installed throughout the designed landscape. If only 50% of the designed landscape includes these measures, then only 50% of the points are available.

3. **D.** WE 3, Indoor Water Use, Very High Efficiency Fixtures and Fittings can be met by implementing one or more requirements for very high efficiency fixtures or fittings.

4. **C.** This credit, together with SS 2.5, is a performance-based alternative to the prescriptive measures in SS 2.2, 2.3, and 2.4 as well as WE 2.1 and 2.2. Project that use the performance approach cannot earn points for prescriptive measures SS 2.2, 2.3 and 2.4 or WE 2.1 and 2.2.

5. **B, C.** WE 2.2, Third-Party Inspection, requires performance of a third-party inspection of the irrigation system in operation, including observation of all of the following: a) all spray heads are operating and delivering water only to intended zones; b) any switches or shut-off valves ware working properly; c) any timers or controllers are set properly; d) any irrigation systems are located at least 2 feet from the home; and, e) irrigation spray does not hit the home.

ENERGY & ATMOSPHERE

1. **A, C.** EA 8, Advanced Lighting, requires installation of ENERGY STAR labeled lamps in 80% of the fixtures throughout the homes. ENERGY STAR labeled CFLs are acceptable. All ceiling fans must be ENERGY STAR labeled.

2. **A.** The mandatory minimum level of energy performance in the LEED for Homes Rating System requires that a qualifying home be designed to meet the energy performance requirements of the ENERGY STAR for Homes program. Under this prerequisite, compliance must be demonstrated using a HERS-approved energy analysis software program.

3. **B.** EA 1 is a performance pathway that requires the builder to use an approved energy analysis software program to demonstrate the overall energy performance of the home's design. Homes built without air-conditioning should be modeled under EA 1, using the default (minimum efficiency allowed) in both the reference and the rated homes.

4. **D.** An ENERGY STAR qualified home is designed to use 15% to 20% less energy than a comparable home built to the 2004 IECC standard

5. **A, C.** To comply with EA 1.1 and 1.2, the Green Rater must complete the verification requirements for an ENERGY STAR home, including thermal bypass (insulation) inspection, envelope air leakage testing with a blower door, and duct leakage testing with a duct pressurization fan. The Green Rater must also visually verify all energy-consuming systems and energy-saving components (e.g., HVAC equipment, windows, insulation, appliances) at the home site. They must also conduct the necessary modeling to produce a HERS index, and include a copy of the HERS rating report.

MATERIALS & RESOURCES

1. **A.** Qualifying materials have one or more of the following attributes: a) FSC-certified wood products, or recycled or reclaimed content; b) low or no emissions of volatile organic compounds (VOCs); and, c) local production (the product was extracted, processed and manufactured within 500 miles of the site.

2. **A.** According to MR 1.4, Framing Efficiencies, efficient framing can be accomplished by using structural insulated panels (SIPs) for walls, roof, or floors.

3. **C.** Best practice for reducing the framing order waste factor is to create a detailed framing order and cut list, as per MR 1.2 and 1.3.

4. **D.** The measure Local Production of Environmentally Preferable Products requires use of products that were extracted, processed, and manufactured within 500 miles of the home.

5. **B.** MR 3, Waste Management, states that construction waste can be reduced or diverted from new construction activities from landfills and incinerators to a level below the industry norm.

INDOOR ENVIRONMENTAL QUALITY

1. **B.** Perform a third-party test of each exhaust air flow rate for compliance with the requirements in section 5 of ASHRAE 62.2-2007.

2. **B.** EQ 8.3, Preoccupancy Flush, can be achieved by flushing the house with windows open for at least 48 hours. In this case, all HVAC fans (including local exhaust) should be run at their maximum air flow for the full 48 hours, and additional internal fans should be used to circulate air.

3. **D.** EQ 2 requires that a CO_2 monitor be installed on each floor of the house and EQ 10.2 requires that potentially one more needs to be installed in the room adjacent to the garage.

4. **A.** EQ 7.1 – 7.3 suggests working with the HVAC contractor to choose an air filter that is suitable to the furnace. It is important that the system is designed with the filter in mind.

5. **C.** Electronic filters cannot be MERV rated, so it is impossible to evaluate their effectiveness.

AWARENESS & EDUCATION

1. **A.** The intent of AE 1 is to maintain the performance of the home by education the occupants about the operations and maintenance of the home's LEED features and equipment.

2. **B.** According to AE 2, Education of Building Manager, signing the Accountability Form indicates that a walk-through has been conducted with the building manager.

3. **B.** According to AE1.2, Enhanced Training, two additional hours are needed to count as enhanced training for occupants of the home.

CREDIT REVIEW SHEET

Test your knowledge of individual credits. Make several printed copies of this sheet, then fill in the blanks from memory for each credit you want to practice.

CATEGORY: _____ NUMBER: _____   AVAILABLE POINTS: _____

NAME: _____

EXEMPLARY PERFORMANCE: _____

TIME : _____ TEAM: _____

INTENT:

_____

_____

REQUIREMENTS:

_____

_____

IMPLEMENTATION STRATEGIES:

_____

_____

STANDARDS:

_____

_____

VERIFICATION & SUBMITTALS:

_____

_____

DOCUMENTATION & CALCULATIONS:

_____

_____

NOTES:

_____

_____

PRIMARY BENEFITS:

_____

_____

ACRONYMS AND ORGANIZATIONS

ACCA	Air Conditioning Contractors of America
AE	Awareness & Education Section
AFUE	Annual Fuel Utilization Efficiency
ALP	ENERGY STAR Advanced Lighting Package
AP	LEED Accredited Professional
ASHRAE	American Society of Heating, Refrigerating and Air-Conditioning Engineers
ASME	American Society of Mechanical Engineers
ASTM	American Society for Testing and Materials
CAE	Combined Annual Efficiency
CFA	Conditioned Floor Area
CFC	Chlorofluorocarbon
CFL	Compact Fluorescent Light
cfm	cubic feet per minute
CFR	U.S. Code of Federal Regulations
CIR	Credit Interpretation Request
CO	Carbon Monoxide
COC	Chain-of-Custody
COP	Coefficient of Performance
CRI	The Carpet and Rug Institute
CZ	Climate Zone
DHW	Domestic Hot Water
DOE	U.S. Department of Energy
DU	Distribution Uniformity
EA	Energy & Atmosphere Section
EER	Energy Efficiency Rating
EERE	U.S. Office of Energy Efficiency and Renewable Energy
EF	Energy Factor
EPA	U.S. Environmental Protection Agency
EQ	Indoor Environmental Quality section
ET	Evapotranspiration
FEMA	U.S. Federal Emergency Management Agency
FSC	Forest Stewardship Council
GBCI	Green Building Certification Institute
gpf	gallons per flush
gpm	gallons per minute
HCFC	Hydrochlorofluorocarbon
HEPA	High-Efficiency Particle Absorbing
HERS	Home Energy Rating System
HET	High-Efficiency Toilet

HOA	Homeowners Association
HSPF	Heating Season Performance Factor
HVAC	Heating, Ventilation and Air Conditioning
IAP	ENERGY STAR with Indoor airPLUS (formerly ENERGY STAR with Indoor Air Package)
IAQ	Indoor Air Quality
ICF	Insulated Concrete Form
ID	Innovation and Design Section
IDR	Innovation and Design Process Request
IECC	International Energy Conservation Code
IRC	International Residential Code
kW	kilowatt
kWh	kilowatt-hour
LED	Light-Emitting Diode
LEED	Leadership in Energy and Environmental Design
LL	Location & Linkages Section
MEF	Modified Energy Factor
MERV	Minimum Efficiency Reporting Value
MR	Materials & Resources Section
NFRC	National Fenestration Rating Council
OSB	Oriented-Strand Board
RESNET	Residential Energy Services Network
SCS	Scientific Certification Systems
SEER	Seasonal Energy Efficiency Rating
SHGC	Solar Heat Gain Coefficient
SIP	Structural Insulated Panel
SRI	Solar Reflectance Index
SS	Sustainable Sites Section
TASC	Technical Advisory Sub-Committee
UL	Underwriters Laboratories
USGBC	U.S. Green Building Council
VOC	Volatile Organic Compound
WE	Water Efficiency Section
WF	Water Factor
WFA	Window-To-Floor Area Ratio

EXEMPLARY PERFORMANCE MATRIX

Exemplary performance strategies may be the result of performance that greatly exceeds the performance level that is required in a home. To earn exemplary performance credits, project teams must meet the performance level defined by the next step in the threshold progression.

CREDIT	EXEMPLARY PERFORMANCE ELIGIBILITY	THRESHOLD
INNOVATION & DESIGN		
ID 3: Innovative or Regional Design	All exemplary performance points earned under other credits must be scored under this credit.	N/A
LOCATION & LINKAGES		
LL 5 : Community Resources / Transit	Projects can earn 1 ID point if they are within ½ mile of transit services that offer 250 or more transit rides per weekday.	250 rides per weekday
SUSTAINABLE SITES		
SS 2.5: Reduce Irrigation Demand by at Least 20%	Projects can earn 1 ID point if the requirements of SS 2.2, parts (b), (c), and (d) are met. This exemplary performance point is only available on projects that use measure SS 2.5.	Meet SS 2.2 parts b, c, and d
SS3: Reduce Heat Island Effects	Projects can earn ½ ID point if 100% of the sidewalks, patios, and driveways meet the credit requirements.	100%
SS 5: Nontoxic Pest Control	Projects that implement nontoxic pest control measures beyond the maximum four rewarded in this credit can earn additional points, to be counted under Innovation & Design 3. Each additional measure is worth ½ point, with a maximum of 1 exemplary performance point total. Not all projects can take advantage of exemplary points for this measure. Projects that are in "moderate to heavy" through "very heavy" on the termite infestation probability map in the LEED for Homes Reference Guide, 2008, are the only projects that can earn exemplary performance points.	5 control measures.
SS 6: Compact Development	Projects with a density greater than 40 dwelling units per acre of buildable land may submit a request for an exemplary performance point through their LEED for Homes Certification Provider.	40 dwelling units per acre.
WATER EFFICIENCY		
WE 1.1: Rainwater Harvesting System	Projects that install a system sized to capture water from 100% of the roof area and can demonstrate a demand for this water can apply for 1 additional point, to be counted under Innovation & Design 3. This application must be submitted by the Provider and approved by USGBC before the point can be counted.	100%
WE 1.2: Graywater Reuse System	Projects that install a graywater system that collects water from multiple elements (e.g., clothes washers, showers, and wash basin faucets) and can demonstrate a demand for this water can apply for 1 additional point, to be counted under Innovation & Design 3. This application must be submitted by the Provider and approved by USGBC before the point can be counted.	2 elements.

CREDIT	EXEMPLARY PERFORMANCE ELIGIBILITY	THRESHOLD
WE 2.1: High-Efficiency Irrigation System	Projects that implement irrigation measures beyond the maximum 3 points in this credit can earn additional points, to be counted under Innovation & Design 3. Each additional measure is worth 1.2 point, for a maximum of 2 exemplary performance point's total.	7 measures.
WE 2.3: Reduce Overall Irrigation Demand by at Least 45%	Projects can earn ID points for achieving a reduction in estimated outdoor water use for 65% or more. A reduction of 65% or more is awarded 1 ID point; 70% or more is awarded 2 ID points; 75% or more is awarded 3 ID points; 80% or more is awarded 4 ID points.	65%
WE 3: High Efficiency Fixtures & Fittings	Projects that can demonstrate flow rates that are substantially lower than those in WE 3.2 can earn 1 additional point, to be counted under Innovation & Design 3. This application must be submitted by the Provider and approved by USGBC before the point can be counted.	Substantially lower than WE 3.2.

ENERGY & ATMOSPHERE

CREDIT	EXEMPLARY PERFORMANCE ELIGIBILITY	THRESHOLD
EA 4: Windows	Homes that install windows that exceed the performance specification in EA 4.3 should follow the performance pathway (EA 1) to earn credit.	Exceed EQ 4.3.
EA 8.3: Advanced Lighting Package	Projects can earn 1 ID point for the use of 90% ENERGY STAR fixtures (i.e. not just lamps)and 100% ENERGY STAR ceiling fans.	90% hardwired fixtures
EA 9: Appliances	The energy models that are used for the performance pathway (EA 1) do not recognize the benefits of water-efficient clothes washers. A project using the performance pathway can earn exemplary performance points for meeting the requirements in EA 9.1 and 9.2 for close washers (1.5 points total).	Meet EA 9.1 & 9.1 under EA 1 performance pathway.

MATERIALS & RESOURCES

CREDIT	EXEMPLARY PERFORMANCE ELIGIBILITY	THRESHOLD
MR 1: Material-Efficient Framing	Projects that implement advanced framing measures worth more than 3 points can take credit for the additional measures, to be counted under Innovation & Design 3.	4 measures.
MR 2.2: Environmentally Preferable Materials	Projects that use more than 16 of the options in Table 1, Environmentally Preferable Products (page 248). And earn more than the maximum 8 points can ear additional points, to be counted under Innovation & Design 3. Each additional measure is worth 0.5 point, with a maximum of 4 exemplary performance points total.	17 options.
MR 3: Waste Management	Projects that can demonstrate that no waste was created or that 100% of the waste was diverted can earn an additional 0.5 point, to be counted under Innovation & Design 3.	No waste / 100% diversion.

INDOOR ENVIRONMENTAL QUALITY

CREDIT	EXEMPLARY PERFORMANCE ELIGIBILITY	THRESHOLD
EQ 8.2: Indoor Contaminant Control	Projects that implement all three measures in this credit can earn 1 additional point, to be counted under Innovation & Design 3.	3 measures.

AWARENESS & EDUCATION

None

REFERENCE STANDARD TABLE

REFERENCE TITLE	REFERENCE DESCRIPTION
ACCA Manual D	ACCA Manual D: Residential Duct Systems. 1995. Air Conditioning Contractors of America.
ACCA Manual J	ACCA Manual J: Residential Load Calculation. 2006. Air Conditioning Contractors of America.
ACCA Manual S	Residential Heating and Cooling Equipment Selection. 2004. Air Conditioning Contractors of America.
ANSI Z21.88/CSA 2.33-2005	Vented Gas Fireplace Heaters. 2005. American National Standards Institute/ Canadian Standards Association.
ANSI Z765-2003	Method for Calculating Square Footage in Single-family Attached and Detached Homes. 2003. American National Standards Institute.
ASHRAE Handbooks	American Society of Heating, Refrigerating and Air-Conditioning Engineers.
ANSI/ASHRAE Standard 52.2	Method of Testing General Ventilation Air-Cleaning Devices for Removal Efficiency by Particle Size
ANSI/ASHRAE Standard 55-2004	Thermal Environmental Conditions for Human Occupancy. 2004. American Society of Heating, Refrigerating and Air-Conditioning Engineers.
ANSI/ASHRAE Standard 62.2-2007	Ventilation and Acceptable Indoor Air Quality in Low-Rise Residential Buildings. 2007. American Society of Heating, Refrigerating and Air-Conditioning Engineers.
ANSI/ASHRAE Standard 152-2004	Method of Test for Determining the Design and Seasonal Efficiencies of Residential Thermal Distribution Systems. 2004. American Society of Heating, Refrigerating and Air-Conditioning Engineers.
ASTM Standard E1465-06	Standard Practice for Radon Control Options for the Design and Construction of New Low-Rise Residential Buildings. 2006. American Society for Testing and Materials.
ASTM Standard E1509-04	Standard Specification for Room Heaters, Pellet Fuel-Burning Type. 2004. American Society for Testing and Materials.
ASTM Standard E1554-03	Standard Test Methods for Determining External Air Leakage of Air Distribution Systems by Fan Pressurization. 2003. American Society for Testing and Materials.
ASTM Standard E1602-03	Standard Guide for Construction of Solid Fuel Burning Masonry Heaters. 2003. American Society for Testing and Materials.
ASTM E2121-03	Standard Practice for Installing Radon Mitigation Systems in Existing Low-Rise Residential Buildings.
ASTM Standard E2136-01	Standard Guide for Specifying and Evaluating Performance of Single-family Attached and Detached Dwellings—Durability. 2001. American Society for Testing and Materials.
ASTM Standard E2600-08	Standard Practice for Assessment of Vapor Intrusion into Structures on Property Involved in Real Estate Transactions. 2008. American Society for Testing and Materials.
California Section 01350	Special Environmental Requirements Specification, including Addendum 2004-1: Standard Practice for the Testing of Volatile Organic Emissions from Various Sources Using Small-Scale Environmental Chambers. 2004. State of California.

REFERENCE TITLE	REFERENCE DESCRIPTION
CABO	CABO One and Two Family Dwelling Code. 1998. Council of American Building Officials.
California Energy Commission, Title 24, ACM RESIDENTIAL MANUAL APPENDIX RD-2005	Procedure for Determining Refrigerant Charge in cooling equipment.
California Graywater Systems, Title 24, Part 5, CA Administrative Code	These standards include code requirements, details, and systems design standards for installation of graywater systems.
CRI Green Label Plus	Carpet and Rug Institute Green Label Testing Programs.
CSA S478-95	CSA Standard S478-95 (R-2001): Guideline on Durability in Buildings. 2001. Canadian Standards Association.
Energy Policy Act 1992	Mandated the use of water-conserving plumbing fixtures and fittings.
ENERGY STAR HVAC QI	ENERGY STAR HVAC Quality Installation (pilot program). U.S. Environmental Protection Agency.
ENERGY STAR Labeled Lighting	Standards for energy efficient lighting.
ENERGY STAR Qualified Appliances	Standards for energy efficient residential appliances.
ENERGY STAR Thermal Bypass Checklist	U.S. Environmental Protection Agency.
EPA/600/R-04/121A	EPA's Storm Water Best Management Practice Design Guide (EPA/600/R-04/121). 2004. U.S. Environmental Protection Agency.
EPA Building Radon Out	Building Radon Out: A Step-by-Step Guide on How to Build Radon-Resistant Homes. 2001. U.S. Environmental Protection Agency.
EPA Heat Island Effect	Basic information about heat island effect. www.epa.gov/heatisland
EPA Radon Maps	EPA's Map of Radon Zones. 2008. U.S. Environmental Protection Agency.
EPA Standard for New Residential Wood Heaters	40 CFR Part 60, subpart AAA: Standards of Performance for New Residential Wood Heaters. 1988. U.S. Environmental Protection Agency.
EPA Vapor Intrusion Primer	Brownfields Technology Primer: Vapor Intrusion Considerations for Redevelopment. 2008. U.S. Environmental Protection Agency.
EPA WaterSense Program	www.epa.gov/WaterSense/
FSC	The Forestry Stewardship Council (FSC) certifies forestry management practices.
FSC COC	The FSC Chain-of-custody (COC) process enables the tracking of wood that originates in FSC-certified forests all the way through to the value chain into final products.
Green Seal Standard GS-11	GS-11: Green Seal Environmental Standard for Paints and Coatings. 2008. Green Seal, Inc.
Green Seal Standard GS-43	Green Seal Environmental Standard for Recycled Latex Paint. 2006. Green Seal, Inc.

REFERENCE TITLE	REFERENCE DESCRIPTION
Greenguard Certification for Paints and Coatings	Paints and Coatings. 2005. Greenguard Environmental Institute.
HERS Insulation Installation Grades	Standards for grading insulation installation.
Home Energy Rating System (HERS) Index	A system for evaluating the energy efficiency of a home using an energy simulation model.
IBC	International Building Code. 2003. International Code Council, Inc.
IBC 2112.1	International Building Code Chapter 21, Masonry. Definition of Masonry Heaters. 2003. International Code Council, Inc.
IECC	International Energy Conservation Code. 2004. International Code Council, Inc.
IECC	International Energy Conservation Code. 2006. International Code Council, Inc.
IECC 502.1.3	International Energy Conservation Code. Recessed Lighting Fixtures. 2001. International Code Council, Inc.
IRC	International Residential Code for One- and Two-Family Dwellings. 2006. International Code Council, Inc.
Maximum Performance (MaP™) TESTING California Urban Water Conservation Council	A testing protocol for toilet performance.
NFPA 54	National Fuel Gas Code. 2006. National Fire Protection Association.
NFPA 720	Standard for the Installation of Household Carbon Monoxide (CO) Warning Equipment. 2005. National Fire Protection Association.
NFRC	National Fenestration Rating Council administers a rating and labeling system for energy performance of windows.
RESNET	Mortgage Industry National Home Energy Rating System Standards. 2006. Residential Energy Services Network.
SCAQMD Rule 1113	Standard for Architectural Coatings. 2007. South Coast Air Quality Management District.
SCAQMD Rule 1168	Standard for Low-Emissions Adhesives and Sealants, South Coast Air Quality Management District.
UL 127	Standard for Factory-Built Fireplaces. 1996. Underwriters Laboratories, Inc.
UL 181A	Standard for Closure Systems for Use with Rigid Air Ducts. 2005. Underwriters Laboratories, Inc.
UL 181B	Standard for Closure Systems for Use with Flexible Air Ducts and Air Connectors. 2005. Underwriters Laboratories, Inc.
UL 1482	Standard for Solid-Fuel Type Room Heaters. 1996. Underwriters Laboratories, Inc.
UL 2034	Standard for Single and Multiple Station Carbon Monoxide Alarms. 1996. Underwriters Laboratories, Inc.
Universal Plumbing Code	Standard used throughout the United States for procedures designed to provide consumers with safe and sanitary plumbing systems.
WAC 173-433-100 (3)	Washington State Code, Chapter 173-433: Solid Fuel Burning Devices, Section 100 (3): Emissions Performance

LEED FOR HOMES SIMPLIFIED PROJECT CHECKLIST

The LEED for Homes Checklist documents that all prerequisites and applicable credits were achieved by the project. A signed checklist is the first of four documents required in the submittal package. (The other three documents are the Accountability Form, the Durability Risk Evaluation Form, and the durability inspection checklist.) The LEED for Homes Checklist tracks the project's progress and includes built-in automated calculators. It constitutes part one of the submittal.

for Homes

LEED for Homes Simplified Project Checklist

Builder Name:	
Project Team Leader (if different):	
Home Address (Street/City/State):	

Project Description:

Building type:

\# of bedrooms: **0**

Project type:

Floor area: **0**

Adjusted Certification Thresholds

Certified: **45.0**		Gold: **75.0**	
Silver: **60.0**		Platinum: **90.0**	

Project Point Total	Final Credit Category Total Points			
Prelim: *0 + 0 maybe pts* Final: *0*	ID: *0* SS: *0*	EA: *0*		EQ: *0*
Certification Level	LL: *0* WE: *0*	MR: *0*		AE: *0*
Prelim: *Not Certified* Final: *Not Certified*	*Min. Point Thresholds Not Met for Prelim. OR Final Rating*			

date last updated :

last updated by :

				Max Points	Preliminary Y/Pts	Maybe	No	Final Y/Pts
Innovation and Design Process (ID)			(No Minimum Points Required)	Max	Y/Pts	Maybe	No	Y/Pts
1. Integrated Project Planning	1.1	Preliminary Rating		Prereq				
	1.2	Integrated Project Team		1	0	0		0
	1.3	Professional Credentialed with Respect to LEED for Homes		1	0	0		0
	1.4	Design Charrette		1	0	0		0
	1.5	Building Orientation for Solar Design		1	0	0		0
2. Durability Management Process	2.1	Durability Planning		Prereq				
	2.2	Durability Management		Prereq				
	2.3	Third-Party Durability Management Verification		3	0	0		0
3. Innovative or Regional Design	3.1	Innovation #1		1	0	0		0
	3.2	Innovation #2		1	0	0		0
	3.3	Innovation #3		1	0	0		0
	3.4	Innovation #4		1	0	0		0
		Sub-Total for ID Category:		**11**	0	0		0
Location and Linkages (LL)		(No Minimum Points Required)	OR	Max	Y/Pts	Maybe	No	Y/Pts
1. LEED ND	1	LEED for Neighborhood Development	LL2-6	10	0	0		0
2. Site Selection	2	Site Selection		2	0	0		0
3. Preferred Locations	3.1	Edge Development	LL 3.2	1	0	0		0
	3.2	Infill		2	0	0		0
	3.3	Previously Developed		1	0	0		0
4. Infrastructure	4	Existing Infrastructure		1	0	0		0
5. Community Resources/ Transit	5.1	Basic Community Resources / Transit	LL 5.2, 5.3	1	0	0		0
	5.2	Extensive Community Resources / Transit	LL 5.3	2	0	0		0
	5.3	Outstanding Community Resources / Transit		3	0	0		0
6. Access to Open Space	6	Access to Open Space		1	0	0		0
		Sub-Total for LL Category:		**10**	0	0		0
Sustainable Sites (SS)		(Minimum of 5 SS Points Required)	OR	Max	Y/Pts	Maybe	No	Y/Pts
1. Site Stewardship	1.1	Erosion Controls During Construction		Prereq				
	1.2	Minimize Disturbed Area of Site		1	0	0		0
2. Landscaping	2.1	No Invasive Plants		Prereq				
	2.2	Basic Landscape Design	SS 2.5	2	0	0		0
	2.3	Limit Conventional Turf	SS 2.5	3	0	0		0
	2.4	Drought Tolerant Plants	SS 2.5	2	0	0		0
	2.5	Reduce Overall Irrigation Demand by at Least 20%		6	0	0		0
3. Local Heat Island Effects	3	Reduce Local Heat Island Effects		1	0	0		0
4. Surface Water Management	4.1	Permeable Lot		4	0	0		0
	4.2	Permanent Erosion Controls		1	0	0		0
	4.3	Management of Run-off from Roof		2	0	0		0
5. Nontoxic Pest Control	5	Pest Control Alternatives		2	0	0		0

LEED FOR HOMES ACCOUNTABILITY FORM

This form is to be completed by the person/organization responsible for the design and/or implementation of one or more of the LEED for Homes credits. This form is used when verification of a specific credit is beyond the ability of the LEED for Homes Green Rater. The Accountability Form constitutes part two of the submittal package.

Project Information	
Home Address:	Return to:
Builder:	

Areas of Accountability

Innovation and Design Process (ID)	Responsible Party	initial
ID 3.1 Innovation #1:		
ID 3.2 Innovation #2:		
ID 3.3 Innovation #3:		
ID 3.4 Innovation #4:		

Location & Linkages (LL)	Responsible Party	initial
LL 2. Site Selection: None of the buildings, built structures, roads, or parking areas are located on portions of sites that meet any of the following criteria: a) land whose elevation is at or below 100-year floodplain defined by FEMA; b) land identified as habitat for any species on the threatened or endangered lists; c) land within 100 feet of any water, including wetlands; d) land that was public parkland prior to the project, unless land of equal or greater value as parkland is accepted in trade by the public landowner; e) land that contains "prime soils", "unique soils", or "soils of state significance".		

Sustainable Sites (SS)	Responsible Party	initial
SS 2.1 No Invasive Plants: No invasive plant species introduced into the landscape.		
SS 2.2 Basic Landscape Design: All of the following requirements are met for all designed landscape softscapes: a) any turf must be drought-tolerant; b) do not use turf in densely shaded areas; c) do not use turf in areas with a slope of 25%; d) add mulch or soil amendments as appropriate; e) all compacted soil (e.g., from construction vehicles) should be tilled to at least 6 inches.		
SS 2.3 Limit Conventional Turf: The use of any turf that requires regular mowing, watering and/or chemicals is limited, as indicated below:	*initial only appropriate choice(s) below*	
(1 pt) - less than 60% of designed landscape softscapes		
(2 pts) - less than 40% of designed landscape softscapes		
(3 pts) - less than 20% of designed landscape softscapes		
SS 2.4 Drought Tolerant Plants: Drought-tolerant plantings were chosen:	*initial only appropriate choice(s) below*	
(1 pt) - more than 45% of installed plants are drought-tolerant		
(2 pts) - more than 90% of installed plants are drought-tolerant		
SS 2.5 Reduce Overall Irrigation Demand: Overall outdoor water use was reduced by at least 20% and demonstrated using the method prescribed in the Rating System. All information in the submitted calculations related to outdoor water use is accurate.		
SS 3 Local Heat Island Effects, part (a): Landscaping is designed with trees or vegetated overhangs that shade at least 50% of sidewalks, patios, and driveways within 50 feet of the home at noon on June 21st.		
SS 4.1 Permeable Lot: Lot is designed such that at least 70% of the built environment, not including area under roof, is permeable or designed to capture water runoff for infiltration on-site.	*initial only appropriate choice(s) below*	
(1 pt) - more than 70% of built environment (excluding area under roof) is permeable		
(2 pts) - more than 80% of built environment (excluding area under roof) is permeable		
(3 pts) - more than 90% of built environment (excluding area under roof) is permeable		
(4 pts) - 100% of built environment (excluding area under roof) is permeable		
SS 4.3 Management of Runoff from Roof, part (d): The site is designed by a licensed or certified landscape design or engineering professional such that all water runoff from the home is managed through on-site design elements.		

Water Efficiency (WE)	Responsible Party	initial
WE 2.1 High Efficiency Irrigation Systems: High-efficiency irrigation system elements are installed (measures not listed below do not require an Accountability Form):	*initial only appropriate choice(s) below*	
b) Design and install an irrigation system with head-to-head coverage.		
d) Install a submeter for the irrigation system.		
f) Create separate zones for each type of bedding area based on watering needs.		
g) Install a timer or controller that activates the valves for each watering zone at the best time of		
h) Install pressure-regulating devices to maintain optimal pressure and prevent misting.		
i) Utilize high-efficiency nozzles with an average distribution uniformity (DU) of at least 0.70.		
j) Check valves in heads.		
k) Install a moisture sensor controller or rain delay controller.		
WE 2.3 Reduce Overall Irrigation Demand: Overall outdoor water use was reduced by at least 45% and demonstrated using the method prescribed in the Rating System. All information in the submitted calculations related to outdoor water use is accurate.		

LEED FOR HOMES DURABILITY RISK EVALUATION FORM:

The Durability Risk Evaluation (DRE) Form is used to identify and record all moderate- and high-risk durability issues for the building enclosure, as indicated by the builder.

LEED for Homes
Durability Evaluation Form
(for prerequisite ID 2.1)

Builder Name:	
Project Team Leader:	
Home Address (Street/City/State):	

Home

Building type:	Floor Area:	Structure type:
Project type:	# of Bedrooms:	Exterior roofing:
Number of stories:	Number of full bathrooms:	Garage:

Site

EPA Radon Zone:	Type of soil:
Terrain / topography:	Depth of soil to bedrock:
Predominant landscaping:	Depth of ground water below structure:
Common regional pests:	Proximity to bodies of water?
Other significant features:	Above FEMA 100-year floodplain?
Additional comments:	

Climate

IECC 2004 Climate Zone:	Annual rainfall (inches/yr):
Heating degree days (HDD):	Annual maximum wind speed (mph):
Cooling degree days (CDD):	Avg annual solar radiation (kWh/m^2/day):

Natural disaster risks:
☐ hurricanes ☐ earthquakes ☐ wildfires
☐ tornados ☐ floods ☐ blizzards

Issues

Issue Type	Risk Level		Issue Type	Risk Level
Exterior water:			Pests:	
Interior moisture:			Heat loss:	
Air infiltration:			Ultraviolet radiation:	
Interstitial condensation:			Other: _____	

U.S. Green Building Council

10/21/2009

LEED FOR HOMES DURABILITY INSPECTION CHECKLIST:

The durability inspection checklist is used to record all durability strategies being used to mitigate the risks listed in the DRE form; indicate their location in the project documents and record their completion. These two documents constitute part three of the submittal package.

Durability Inspection Checklist Template
(for prerequisite ID 2.1 & 2.2 and credit ID 2.3)

Builder Name:
Project Team Leader:
Home Address:

For each risk type below, list the durability strategies used in the home to help mitigate those risks. For each of the high and moderate risk areas indicated in the Risk Evaluation Form, please include at least three strategies. Where necessary, add additional rows. Refer to the Example Durability Strategies page for sample strategies that may be applicable.

Have the builder or trade indicate where the strategy is included in the drawings, specification, or scopes of work, and then sign-off that the durability strategies were incorporated into the home. If ID 2.3 is being pursued, have the Green Rater sign-off that the strategies were verified in the home.

Durability Strategies by Issue Type	Location in Drawings, Specifications, and/or Scopes of Work	Sign-off by Responsible Party (initial below)	
		Prerequisite ID 2.2 (Builder/trade)	Credit ID 2.3 (Green Rater)
Exterior Water / Moisture			
Interior Water / Moisture			
Air Infiltration			
Interstitial Condensation			
Pests			
Heat Loss			
Ultraviolet Radiation			
Natural Disasters			
Other			
Builder Declaration for ID prerequisite 2.1 & 2.2			

I hereby declare and affirm to USGBC that I have evaluated this project's durability risks, completed the Durability Risk Evaluation Form, and incorporated appropriate durability measures into the design to adequately address the moderate and high risks. The construction drawings and specifications have been updated accordingly, and the the measures were verified to be completed appropriately.	Name: _____ Title: _____ Signature: _____ Date: _____